Diana Goodey   Noel Goodey   Meredith Levy

Messages

Student's Book

4

CAMBRIDGE
UNIVERSITY PRESS

		Grammar and Expressions	Vocabulary and Pronunciation	Listening and Reading skills	Communicative tasks
Module 1 People and places	**Unit 1 Getting together**	• Describing the present and the past • Verbs + prepositions in *Wh-*questions • Present continuous • *Expressions*: contradictions	• Verbs + prepositions • Postcards • Words with *some* and *every* • *Pronunciation*: stress and intonation	• Listen to biographies of famous people • Read holiday postcards • Skim and scan a text • *Life and culture*: Welcome to Liverpool!	• Talk about a picture • Write about famous people in the past • Make a conversation at a café • Write a postcard
	Unit 2 Friends and neighbours	• Relative clauses with *who, that, which* • Present simple • Pronoun *one/ones* • *Expressions*: asking for clarification	• Flats and houses • Friendship • Nouns and adjectives describing personal qualities • *Pronunciation*: /ə/	• Listen to a guessing game • Read a questionnaire about friendship • Understand new words • *Life and culture*: Poem	• Talk about where you live • Tell the class about yourself and your neighbourhood • Play a guessing game • Write about yourself and friendships in your life
	Review	*Grammar check* *Study skills*: Spelling *How's it going?*: Progress check *Coursework*: Who's who at Greenside?			
Module 2 New horizons	**Unit 3 All in the mind**	• Past continuous and past simple • *used to* • *Expressions*: expressing surprise	• Fears and fantasies • Dreams • Link words • *Pronunciation*: /j/	• Listen to three conversations about coincidences • Read a magazine article about dreams • Identify the topic of a text • *Life and culture*: Haunted Britain	• Talk and write about coincidences in the past • Describe yourself when you were younger and compare with a friend • Describe things that you imagine or worry about • Write a description of a dream
	Unit 4 Journeys	• *must/mustn't, have to/don't have to* • Comparative adjectives • Passive (present simple and past simple) • *Expressions*: making travel arrangements	• On the road • Travelling • Prepositions of movement • *Pronunciation*: stress in sentences	• Listen to a song • Read an account of a journey around the world • Scan a text for information • *Life and culture*: Journey into slavery	• Write and act a conversation at a travel agent's • Describe where things are/were made or produced • Write a journal about a journey
	Review	*Grammar check* *Study skills*: Guessing what words mean *How's it going?*: Progress check *Coursework*: Conversation with Grace Lawson			
Module 3 Changes	**Unit 5 In the news**	• Present perfect + *just, yet, already* • *been* and *gone* • Present perfect and past simple • *its*: possessive adjective • *so ... that ... ; such a/an ... that ...* • *Expressions*: offers and suggestions	• Topics in the news • Yellowstone Park • *Pronunciation*: /s/ + consonant	• Listen to news headlines on the radio • Read a magazine article about a volcano • Understand the main idea of a text • *Life and culture*: Non-stop news	• Write an email to a friend or relative with your news • Discuss what you have and haven't done • Write a radio report • Write about recent events for a school newsletter
	Unit 6 Attachments	• Present perfect with *for* and *since* • Present perfect with superlative adjective + *ever* • Superlative adjectives • *give* + direct and indirect object • *Expressions*: time expressions	• Personal possessions • Living abroad • *still, any more* • *Pronunciation*: /ɜː/ /ɔː/	• Listen to an interview with a surfing champion • Read an interview with a boy who has lived all over the world • Skim a text for the general idea • *Life and culture*: New Zealand	• Give details about your background • Talk about your favourite possessions • Describe important things and events • Write an account of personal experiences
	Review	*Grammar check* *Study skills*: Homophones *How's it going?*: Progress check *Coursework*: Reviews			

		Grammar and Expressions	Vocabulary and Pronunciation	Listening and Reading skills	Communicative tasks
Module 4 Talking points	**Unit 7** Celebrations	• First conditional with *if* and *unless* • The future with *will* and *going to* • *Expressions*: I hope so/not. I guess so/not.	• Special occasions • Invitations and replies • Verbs with *look* • *Pronunciation*: final /s/ and /z/	• Listen to a song • Read invitations and replies • Scan a text for information • *Life and culture*: The number 13	• Describe special occasions • Talk about superstitions • Write about and discuss plans for a celebration • Write and reply to an invitation
	Unit 8 Secrets and lies	• *might* and *may* • *when* in future sentences • *should/shouldn't* • Second conditional • *Expressions*: responding to opinions	• Verbs and nouns that go together • 'Sales talk' • *because, so* • *Pronunciation*: /aɪ/ /eɪ/	• Listen to a discussion on the radio • Read an article about a 'con man' • Predict the topic of a text • *Life and culture*: The code talkers	• Talk about events in the future and when they might happen • Talk about what's right and wrong • Write an imaginary 'sales talk'
	Review	*Grammar check* *Study skills*: Preparing for tests and exams		*How's it going?*: Progress check	*Coursework*: Letters
Module 5 Living together	**Unit 9** Groups	• Verb/preposition + *-ing* form • *-ing* form and *to* + verb • *want/ask/tell* someone to do something • *Expressions*: requests and responses	• People in groups • A wildlife commentary • *too* and *enough* • *Pronunciation*: /ŋ/ /n/	• Listen to phone calls making requests • Read a commentary for a TV wildlife programme • Use pronouns and possessive adjectives • *Life and culture*: Romeo and Juliet	• Describe people's likes and dislikes • Interview a friend for a TV show • Write and act a telephone conversation asking someone to do something • Write a description of teenagers in your country
	Unit 10 Food for thought	• Expressions of quantity • Question words • Subject and object questions • *Expressions*: expressing preferences	• Food • The fast food industry • Adjectives ending in *-ed/-ing* • *Pronunciation*: silent vowels	• Listen to a TV quiz programme • Read a review of a book • Recognise facts and opinions • *Life and culture*: Make Poverty History	• Talk about things you'd like to change • Prepare and ask questions for a quiz • Write a review for a school magazine
	Review	*Grammar check* *Study skills*: Preparing and giving a talk		*How's it going?*: Progress check	*Coursework*: The ads page
Module 6 Just imagine!	**Unit 11** Challenges	• Past perfect • *must, can't, might, could* for speculation • *Expressions*: Neither do I. So am I.	• Adjectives describing feelings • In the mountains • Adverbs • *Pronunciation*: stress in sentences, weak forms	• Listen to a story about a terrible night • Read a story about an extraordinary experience • Guess meaning from context • *Life and culture*: Gandhi	• Describe a situation in the past and how you felt • Imagine what different situations are like • Write a short story
	Unit 12 Happy endings	• Reported speech • *say* and *tell* • *whose* • *Expressions*: everyday expressions	• Words connected with money • Sending messages • Phrasal verbs • *Pronunciation*: vowel sounds	• Listen to a song • Read three jumbled stories • Follow the sequence of a story • *Life and culture*: Keeping in touch	• Report what people say • Make a conversation at a party • Write and reply to a message
	Review	*Grammar check* *Study skills*: Learning English on your own		*How's it going?*: Progress check	*Coursework*: Sports news

• **Grammar index** • **Communicative functions index** • **Wordlist** • **Phonetic symbols** • **Verb forms and irregular verbs** • **Songs**

Module 1

People and places

In Module 1 Steps 1 and 2 you study

Grammar
- Describing the present and the past
- Verbs + prepositions in *Wh-* questions
- Present continuous
- Relative clauses with *who, that, which*
- Present simple
- Pronoun *one/ones*

Vocabulary
- Verbs + prepositions
- Flats and houses

Expressions
- Contradictions: *Yes, he is! No, he hasn't!*
- Asking for clarification

so that you can
- Talk about a picture
- Write about famous people in the past
- Contradict someone
- Make a conversation about going out with friends
- Talk about where you live
- Describe people and things
- Ask for more information
- Play a guessing game

Life and culture

Welcome to Liverpool!
Poem

Coursework 1

Part 1 Who's who at Greenside?
You write about people who work at your school.

Find out more about the people who work at Greenside

Perhaps you're reading this article in the canteen, while you're eating your lunch. This month we'd like to introduce you to the person who does all the cooking. His name's **Del Stanley**. Del trained to be a chef in London and he came to Greenside College two years ago. He says 'I like using fresh, local food if I can. It isn't always easy to find things that everyone likes – teenagers are very unadventurous when they choose their meals!'

A lot of p
most imp
mends th
at the en
are clean
to-five jo
work in th
some fre
got a bla

In Step 3 you ...

read
- Three postcards
- A questionnaire about friendship

study
- Words beginning with *some* and *every*
- Nouns and adjectives describing personal qualities
- Skimming and scanning a text
- Understanding new words

so that you can
- Write a postcard
- Express your opinions about friendships

What's it about?

What can you say about the pictures?

Now match the pictures with sentences 1–4.

1 The sun's going down and everything looks beautiful.
2 He works in a shop that sells newspapers and food.
3 He's wearing a hat and coat.
4 We live in a flat on the first floor.

Coursework
Our school magazine

In Book 4 you study
● a magazine written by students at Greenside Community College

so that you can
● make an English magazine for people at your school

Your Coursework has got six parts:

Part 1 Who's who at Greenside?
You write about people who work at your school.

Part 2 In conversation with Grace Lawson
You talk to an old person in your neighbourhood and write a short interview.

Part 3 Reviews
You write a review of a book, film or TV programme.

Part 4 Letters to the editor
You write a letter for a magazine letters page.

Part 5 The ads page
You make adverts to put in your school magazine.

Part 6 Sports news
You write a report about a sporting event.

Getting together

In Step 1 you revise
- describing the present and the past

so that you can
- talk about a picture
- write about famous people in the past

1 Share your ideas

Describe the painting. What are the people doing? What do you think of the painting?

> The woman is laughing.

> I like it, but I think it's a sad painting.

2 Reading *Idols of the 20th century*

a Look at the painting and read the description. Find at least:

1 three verbs in the present.
2 three verbs in the past.

The name of the painting is *Nighthawks: Boulevard of Broken Dreams*. It's by an Austrian painter called Gottfried Helnwein. It shows a scene in a diner in the USA during the 1950s. Outside, the street is dark and empty. Inside, three people are sitting at the counter, a woman and two men. A waiter is standing behind the counter. The man in the middle of the picture is wearing a blue suit and tie. He doesn't look very happy. The woman on the right is laughing and talking to the man next to her, but he isn't listening.

The four people in the picture are all famous American stars from the 20th century. The man in the blue suit is the actor Humphrey Bogart. Bogart was born in New York. At first, he acted in the theatre, but for many years he wasn't successful. Then he started working for the Warner film studio and, at the age of 40, he finally became a star. He made more than thirty films. Two of his most famous films were *The African Queen* and *Casablanca*. Bogart died in his sleep at his home in Hollywood in 1957.

b 📻 Listen to the first paragraph and follow in your book. Then find these things.

1 a nationality   2 a country   3 two jobs
4 two things that people wear

c 📻 Listen to the second paragraph and follow in your book. Then copy and complete the fact file.

Fact File • • • • • • • • • • • • • •

Humphrey Bogart, actor, 1899 –[1]..........
Born in: [2]..........
Worked for: [3]..........
Most famous films: [4]..........

4 Listening *Biographies*

Read the two fact files. Then listen to the biographies of Marilyn Monroe and Elvis Presley. Write the missing information in your notebook.

> **Fact File** • • • • • • • • • • • • • •
>
> **Marilyn Monroe, actress, 1926–**[1]_____
> **Born in: Los Angeles**
> [2]_____ **name: Norma Jean Baker**
> **Worked for:** [3]_____ **Century Fox**
> **Most famous film:** *Some Like It* [4]_____

> **Fact File** • • • • • • • •
>
> **Elvis Presley, singer, 19**[5]_____**–1977**
> **Born in: Tupelo, Mississippi**
> **Played the** [6]_____ **from the age of**
> [7]_____
> **Worked for: RCA** [8]_____
> **Most famous hits:** [9]_____ *Be Cruel,*
> *Jailhouse Rock,* [10]_____ *Suede Shoes*

3 Revision *Describing the present and the past*

Look at the painting and complete the description of James Dean.

On the left, there [1]_____ (*be*) a tall, good-looking young man. He [2]_____ (*wear*) a dark coat and a scarf. He looks sad and lonely. He [3]_____ (*not talk*) to anyone. He [4]_____ (*be*) the famous American actor James Dean.

James Dean [5]_____ (*be*) born in Indiana in 1931. At first, he [6]_____ (*act*) on television and, four years later, he [7]_____ (*become*) a film star. But Dean only [8]_____ (*make*) three films. He [9]_____ (*die*) in a car accident in September 1955.

> **Try this!**
> How many words for clothes
> do you know?
> *scarf, ...*

5 Writing *Elvis or Marilyn*

> ### Use what you know
>
> Choose either Elvis Presley or Marilyn Monroe. Describe what he/she is doing in the picture. Then use the notes in your fact file and describe his/her real life.

Revision

In Step 2 you study
- verbs + prepositions in *Wh-* questions
- present continuous
- contradictions: *Yes, he is! No, he hasn't!*

so that you can
- contradict someone
- make a conversation about going out with friends

1 Key vocabulary

Verbs + prepositions

a ⏲ Complete the sentences with the prepositions in the box. You've got three minutes!

about	at	for	from	to

1 I'm often late in the morning because I have to **look** *for* my things.
2 I like **looking** .... my friends' photos.
3 I don't often **think** .... the future.
4 I don't **come** .... this country. I was born abroad.
5 When I'm with my friends, we often **talk** .... films and music.
6 I don't like **waiting** .... people when they're late.
7 In class, I usually **talk** .... my English teacher in English.
8 My father and I **argue** .... football.

🔊 Listen and check.

b What about you? Which of the sentences in 1a are true for you? Work with a friend and tell him/her at least three things about yourself.

> I don't come from this country. I was born in …

2 Presentation *Who are we waiting for?*

a What can you say about the photos?

b 🔊 Close your book and listen to the conversation. What are Danny and his friends doing this evening?

Danny and Nadia live in Liverpool. They're in a café and they're waiting for their friends.

DANNY: What's the time, Nadia?
NADIA: It's nearly half past seven.
DANNY: So who are we waiting for?
NADIA: Clare and Luke. Luke's always late.
DANNY: No, he isn't!
NADIA: Yes, he is! I'll phone him. … Luke, where are you? We're waiting for you.
DANNY: Here's Clare! Hi, Clare.
CLARE: Hi! Sorry I'm late. Who's Nadia talking to?
DANNY: Luke. He's late too. And he's got the tickets.
CLARE: No, he hasn't! I've got them. They're in my bag.
NADIA: Hi, Clare. We must go. It's half past seven.
DANNY: What about Luke?
NADIA: He's meeting us outside the cinema in ten minutes.
DANNY: OK.
NADIA: What are you looking for, Clare?
CLARE: The tickets. I can't find them.
DANNY: You're joking!
CLARE: Hang on! No, we're OK. They're here, in my pocket.

c 🔊 Listen again and follow in your book. Are these sentences true or false? Correct the false sentences.

1 Danny and Nadia are late.
2 Luke's waiting for Danny and Nadia.
3 Danny's talking to Nadia on the phone.
4 Luke has got the tickets.
5 The tickets aren't in Clare's bag.
6 Danny and his friends are meeting Luke at twenty to eight.

3 Key grammar

Verbs + prepositions in Wh- questions

Look at the answers and complete the question.

> Who are they **waiting for**?
> They're waiting for their friends.
> Who's Nadia **talking** ....?
> She's talking to Luke.
>
> *The preposition stays after the verb in these questions.*

G ➤ 26

4 Practice

Make questions for these answers.

1 What are Luke and Clare talking about?

1 They're talking about the film. (*What / Luke and Clare ?*)
2 He's looking at a poster. (*What / Danny ?*)
3 She's listening to the radio. (*What / Clare ?*)
4 He's looking for his mobile. (*What / Luke ?*)
5 She's talking to her boyfriend. (*Who / Nadia ?*)
6 I'm waiting for Clare. (*Who / you ?*)
7 They're arguing about music. (*What / Nadia and Danny ?*)

Remember!

We use the present continuous:

● *to describe things that are in progress now:*
Nadia**'s phoning** Luke.

● *for temporary situations:*
Clare's sister **is working** in Japan at the moment.

● *for arrangements in the future:*
They**'re meeting** Luke in ten minutes.

5 Key expressions   *Contradictions*

a 🔊 Complete the sentences. Then listen and check.

A: You're always late!
B: No, I'm not!
A: Yes, you *..are..* !

A: You've got my bag.
B: No, I haven't!
A: Yes, you .... !

A: You don't understand!
B: Yes, I *..do..* !
A: No, ... !

A: That isn't true!
B: Yes, it .... !
A: .... !

b Work with a friend and practise the dialogues.

6 Key pronunciation   *Stress and intonation*

🔊 Listen and repeat the four arguments.

1 A: You're crazy!   B: <u>No</u>, I'm <u>not</u>!
2 A: Of course I'm listening!   B: <u>No</u>, you <u>aren't</u>!
3 A: You don't care!   B: <u>Yes</u>, I <u>do</u>!
4 A: I often help!   B: <u>No</u>, you <u>don't</u>!

7 Writing and speaking   *At the café*

Use what you know

Work in pairs and make a short conversation like the one in Exercise 2. You're at a café and you're waiting for someone else.

A: Ask about the other person.
B: Ring the other person. Then answer A's question.

> Who are we waiting for?
> Is Julio coming?

In Step 3 you
- read three postcards
- study words beginning with *some* and *every*

so that you can
- write a postcard

1 Share your ideas
Keeping in touch

How often do you write to your friends and family? Do you write letters, postcards, emails or text messages? Which do you prefer, and why?

> I send a lot of text messages.

2 Reading *Hi there!*

a **Reading skills** *Skimming and scanning*

⏱ Read the three postcards quickly. Match the texts with the photos. You've got two minutes!

Now read the texts again and answer the questions.

1 Where are Nick, Sara and Jared?
2 Are the three writers:
  a describing their holiday plans?
  b describing what's happening around them?
  c writing about the things they've done?

b **Comprehension check**

🔊 Listen, and read the postcards again. Then answer the questions.

1 Who are Nick, Sara and Jared writing to? Can you guess?
2 Is Nick writing his card at the beginning or the end of the day?
3 Does Nick want to go back to England?
4 What's the weather like in Moscow?
5 Is Sara going out tomorrow?
6 What country is Jared travelling across?
7 What can he see outside the window?
8 Are the people on the plane laughing and talking?

a

1

1st September

Hi Becky,
This place is incredible! I'm sitting on a rock somewhere in the middle of the Shimba Hills. The sun's going down and everything looks so beautiful. African sunsets are amazing. I'm staying at the Marakibo Travellers' Camp at the moment. There are butterflies everywhere. I love it here and I don't want to come home. Say hello to everyone in the office from me.
All the best,
Nick

2

Tuesday

Dear everyone,
I'm sitting in a café near Red Square, drinking Russian tea! Natasha seems nice. Today she's taking me on a tour of the city. It's really cold so I'm wearing one of Natasha's hats! I look a bit stupid but it's nice and warm. Everything's going OK and Natasha's parents both speak English quite well. We're all going to an ice hockey match tomorrow. I'll ring at the weekend.
Bye for now,
Sara

3

17th April
(or I guess it's the 18th now!)

Hi!
I'm writing this on a plane about halfway between Atlanta and Los Angeles. It's after midnight and nearly everyone's asleep. The lights are low and outside there's a full moon. Behind me someone's listening to music on their headphones and, every few minutes, they sing a bit of the song. It sounds really funny.
I wonder what you're doing right now. I hope you're thinking about me. I miss you.
Love,
Jared

b

c

Moscow

3 Word work someone, everywhere

a Look at the examples.

Someone's listening to music.
There are butterflies **everywhere**.

How many more words can you make with the words in the box?

every	one
some	thing
	where

b Now complete these sentences using words from 3a.

1 Let's have .... to drink.
2 My aunt lives .... in the USA. I'm not sure where.
3 Look at your room! There are clothes .... !
4 There's .... at the door. Is it Clare?
5 There's too much to do. We can't finish .... today.
6 Why don't you walk? You go .... by car!
7 'Where's the station?' 'I don't know. Let's ask ....'
8 Danny's very popular. .... likes him.

Remember!

Every**body**, some**body** *mean the same as* every**one**, some**one**.

Writing guide *Writing a postcard*

● Write the day or date at the top of the card.

  Wednesday
  1st September

● Begin your card with:

  Dear ... or Hi ...!

● Use the present continuous to describe the scene around you.

  I'm sitting ...

● Finish your card with:

  Bye for now, ... / See you soon.
  From ... / Love (from) ...
  Best wishes, ... / All the best, ...

4 Writing *A postcard*

Use what you know

Choose one of the following situations and write a postcard to a friend or someone in your family.

– You're on holiday somewhere special.
– You're staying with a friend abroad.
– You're travelling from one place to another.

Use the Writing guide and the texts in Exercise 2 to help you.

Extra exercises

1 Complete the conversation. Write true answers in reply to these questions.

A: Do you enjoy learning English?
B: ....
A: How many lessons a week do you have?
B: ....
A: Who's your English teacher this term?
B: ....
A: Did you speak any English during the holidays?
B: ....
A: Are you learning any other foreign languages at the moment?
B: ....

2 Choose the right words.

1 What .... Danny and Nadia doing?
   a 's   b does   c are

2 The waiter is .... coffee behind the counter.
   a doing   b making   c makes

3 There's John. .... wearing a blue suit.
   a He's   b She's   c He

4 I can't answer the phone. I .... to send an email.
   a try   b 'm trying   c 's trying

5 .... we going to the cinema this evening?
   a Can   b Are   c Am

6 Luke .... listening! He's asleep!
   a is   b isn't   c 's

3 Read the text and choose the right word(s) for each space.

Marian Boyd [1].......... born in Sydney but she [2].......... live in Australia now. Her family [3].......... to the USA in 2002 and now she [4].......... in New York. [5].......... becoming a successful actress. At the moment [6].......... in a big Broadway theatre, and she sometimes [7].......... on TV.

1 a is   b was   c has
2 a doesn't   b didn't   c isn't
3 a move   b moves   c moved
4 a work   b worked   c 's working
5 a She   b She's   c She was
6 a she acts   b she acted   c she's acting
7 a appears   b appeared   c is appearing

4 Complete the sentences with the right preposition.

1 A: Alan's on the phone to Penny.
   B: What are they talking _about_?
2 A: Have you got a problem?
   B: Yes, I'm looking .... my mobile.
3 A: I can hear Matt. He's in the kitchen.
   B: Who's he talking ....?
4 A: What are you doing here?
   B: I'm waiting .... Lisa.
5 A: What are they arguing ....?
   B: Money, I think.
6 A: Who are you looking ....?
   B: That boy over there. I think he's Paul's brother.

5 Match 1–6 with a–f and make six dialogues.

1 Joe works as a waiter at the George Hotel.
2 You aren't listening to me!
3 Pete's got a new guitar.
4 It's Karen's birthday today.
5 I haven't got time to finish this.
6 He isn't a very good singer.

a No, he hasn't!
b Yes, he is!
c No, it isn't!
d Yes, I am!
e No, he doesn't!
f Yes, you have!

6 How do you say these sentences in your language?

1 Sorry I'm late.
2 It's nice and warm.
3 He looks happy.
4 It sounds funny.
5 You're joking!
6 I wonder what she's doing.

Welcome to Liverpool!

Do you know anything about Liverpool?

My name's Danny Gray and I live in Liverpool. It's in northwest England, on the River Mersey, and it's a great place to live. 'Liverpudlians' are warm, friendly people and we're very proud of our city.

In the nineteenth century, it was an important port and people came here from Ireland, the Caribbean and even China. Today, the population is 450,000 and more than 60 different languages are spoken here.

Liverpool is well known for its football, as you probably know. There are two big clubs, Liverpool and Everton, and the fans are passionate about their team.

Liverpool is often called the UK Capital of Pop. That's because a lot of singers and musicians from Liverpool have had number one hits. I expect you've heard of The Beatles. People called them 'the Fab Four' and, in the 1960s, they became the best-known band in pop history.

Visitors can go on a 'Fab Four tour' and see the four Beatles' old homes, their schools, places in their songs and the Cavern Club, where the group first played. I often go to the Cavern on Friday nights to listen to new bands.

At the weekend, my friends and I sometimes go to the Albert Dock – we look round the shops and have a drink at one of the cafés. There are galleries and museums there too. This weekend my aunt and her family are staying with us. Today, we're taking them to the Museum of Liverpool Life, then we're going on a boat trip on the River Mersey. This evening we're having a Chinese meal at a restaurant in Chinatown.

Why don't you come and visit Liverpool one day?

ABOUT LIVERPOOL SLANG

If you're in Liverpool, a drink is a 'bevvy', and trousers are 'kecks'. And don't say 'goodbye' – say 'ta-ra'!

Task

Read the text, then match 1–5 with a–e and make five true sentences about Liverpool.

1	Liverpool is a city	a	at the Cavern Club.
2	A 'Liverpudlian' is	b	in the north of England.
3	The Mersey	c	came from Liverpool.
4	The Beatles	d	someone from Liverpool.
5	You can hear new bands	e	is a river.

2 Friends and neighbours

STEP 1

In Step 1 you study
- words describing flats and houses
- relative clauses with *who, that, which*
- present simple

so that you can
- talk about where you live
- describe people and things

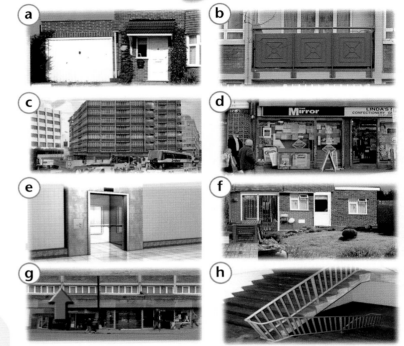

1 Key vocabulary *Flats and houses*

a ⏱ Match the sentences with the pictures. You've got two minutes!

1 Danny lives in a **block of flats**.
2 His family's flat is on the **first floor**.
3 It's got a **balcony**.
4 Danny doesn't usually take the **lift**.
5 He usually goes up the **stairs**.
6 There's a shop on the **ground floor**.
7 There's a **garage** next to Nadia's house.
8 There's a **garden** at the back.

🔊 Listen and check.

b What about you? Ask and answer questions about your home.

> Do you live in a house or a flat?

> What floor is it on?

> Has it got a garden?

Remember!

We use the present simple to describe habits and routines, and things that are generally true:

He **lives** in a flat.
I **don't** usually **take** the lift.

With certain verbs – for example, know, like, want, understand, believe – we use the present simple, not the present continuous.

2 Presentation
The people who live next door

a 🔊 Look at the photos, then listen to Danny and follow in your book. What is Danny's address?

Hi! Welcome to Mandela Court – a block of flats in Liverpool. I live here with my parents and my sister Beth. Our flat is number three, and it's on the first floor at the back. It's got a balcony that overlooks the park. There's a shop on the ground floor which sells newspapers and food. The man who owns the shop is called Karim. I work for him on Saturdays. And I sometimes babysit for the people that live next door. They're called Winston and Lorina. Winston plays the trumpet in a band. They go all over the world. You'll meet some more of our neighbours later …

b Read the text again. Then match 1–6 with a–f and make six sentences.

1 There's a balcony that
2 There's a shop which
3 Danny works for the man who
4 The woman that
5 Danny knows someone who
6 Winston plays in a band that

a sells food.
b has got a view of the park.
c plays in a band.
d lives next door is called Lorina.
e goes all over the world.
f owns the shop.

b Make one sentence each time. Use *who* for people and *that* for things.

1 She works in a shop that sells clothes.

1 She works in a shop. It sells clothes.
2 We've got a balcony. It overlooks the square.
3 Danny's dad has got a friend. He knows the Prime Minister.
4 We've got some neighbours. They come from Brazil.
5 There are several buses. They go to the city centre.

c **Test a friend** Write a sentence from 4b but don't finish it. Can your friend find a new ending?

She works in a shop that sells ... .

> **Try this!**
> Find four nouns, then write definitions with *that* or *who*.
> W_SH_NG M_CH_N_
> H_ _R DRY_R   T_X_ DR_V_R
> D_SC J_CK_Y

3 Key grammar *Relative clauses with* who, that, which

Look at the examples and complete the explanation with *people* and *things*.

> Winston is the man **who/that** lives next door.
> There's a balcony **that/which** overlooks the park.
>
> *In these sentences*, who, that *and* which *are relative pronouns.*
> *We use* who (*and sometimes* that) *for* ....
> *We use* that (*and sometimes* which) *for* ....

G▶ 30

4 Practice

a Match 1–5 with a–e and make five sentences.

1d A shop assistant is a person who works in a shop.

1 A shop assistant is a person who
2 Apollo 11 was a spaceship that
3 A ferry is a boat which
4 A coffee maker is a machine that
5 James Dean was an actor who

a went to the moon.
b carries people and cars.
c died in a car accident.
d works in a shop.
e makes coffee.

5 Key pronunciation /ə/

 Listen and repeat the sentences. Practise the weak form /ə/ in *that*.

1 It's a boat that carries cars.
2 He's the man that lives next door.
3 It's a machine that makes coffee.

6 Writing and speaking
People and things

> **Use what you know**
>
> Complete the sentences about yourself, then tell the class.
>
> We've got a neighbour who ...
> I don't like people who ...
> I live in a house/flat that ...

In Step 2 you study
- *one/ones*
- asking for clarification

so that you can
- ask for more information
- play a guessing game

1 Share your ideas

A lot of teenagers in the UK have got a part-time job. What about young people in your country? Have you got a part-time job?

> My sister works in a restaurant on Saturdays.

2 Presentation *He's the one who goes running*

a 🔲 Look at the photos, then listen to the conversation and follow in your book. Who lives at 7 and 8 Mandela Court?

It's Saturday morning and Danny's at work in Karim's shop. His sister Beth has just come into the shop.

BETH: Hi, Karim. Hi, Danny. Do you sell socks?

DANNY: Yes, we do. They're next to the pet food.

BETH: Oh, yes. They're for Andy. He wants some white ones. And I need a bottle of mineral water.

DANNY: A large one or a small one?

BETH: A small one, please. Thanks, Danny. ... I can't stop. I'm meeting Andy in a minute. See you later. Bye, Karim!

KARIM: Bye, Beth.

DANNY: Bye.

KARIM: Is Andy the one who goes running every morning?

DANNY: Yes. He and Beth are engaged. He lives on the second floor, next door to the Pringles.

KARIM: Who are the Pringles? Are they the ones with the parrot?

DANNY: That's right. They were in the local paper.

KARIM: Ah, yes, I remember. They've got a parrot that can sing.

DANNY: It's really intelligent. It's called Frank. Anyway, we've got another customer. Morning, Winston. How are you today?

b Use the information in the conversation and the photos. Find the names of:

1 two things that Beth wants to buy.
2 someone who goes running.
3 the girl who's going to marry Andy.
4 three people who live on the second floor.
5 a pet that was in the local newspaper.

3 Key grammar one/ones

Read the explanation, then complete the examples.

> *We use* one/ones *when we don't need to repeat a noun:*
> Andy needs some socks. He wants some white ....
> I want a bottle of mineral water. Have you got a small .... ?
>
> *We can also use* the one/ones *with relative pronouns:*
> He's **the one who** goes running.
> They're **the ones that** live next door to Andy.

 31

4 Practice

a Write the sentences again, using *one* or *ones*.

1 *Have you got any black ones?*

1 I need some socks. Have you got any black <u>socks</u>?

2 Which toothbrush is yours? Is it the red <u>toothbrush</u>?

3 We haven't got any large bottles. Is a small <u>bottle</u> OK?

4 Which watch do you prefer – the silver <u>watch</u> or the gold <u>watch</u>?

5 Which shorts do you like – the <u>shorts</u> with pockets or the <u>shorts</u> without pockets?

6 Which is your bedroom – the <u>bedroom</u> that overlooks the garden or the <u>bedroom</u> that overlooks the road?

b If you have time, work with a friend and ask the questions in 4a. Choose your own answer each time.

> I need some socks. Have you got any black ones?

> Yes, we have.

> No, we haven't, but we've got some blue ones.

5 Listening *Which one do you mean?*

a 🔊 Danny and his friends are playing a guessing game. Copy the table, then listen and complete the first column.

	Person, thing or animal?	Clue	Answer
Luke	*animal*	*Australia*	*koala*
Danny			
Nadia			
Clare			

b 🔊 Listen again. Complete the second and third columns with the words in the box.

> kitchen   Australia   Spanish painter   Edison
> microwave   electric light   koala   Dali

6 Key expressions
Asking for clarification

Do you mean the one with the moustache?
Was he the one who painted clocks?
Are they the ones with the parrot?
Which one do you mean?

Work with a friend. Put the conversation in the right order (1–7). *1c*

a No, the one with the moustache is Mr Shapiro.
b Yes, that's right, the one who plays the violin.
c Do you know Mr Morello?
d Because he's going to be on TV tonight.
e Do you mean the one with the big moustache?
f Oh, yes. I know. Anyway, why are you asking?
g Well, who's Mr Morello, then? Is he the one with red curly hair?

🔊 Listen and check, then practise the conversation.

7 Speaking *Can you guess?*

Use what you know

Play the guessing game in Exercise 5.

> It's a building that's in the centre of the town.

> Do you mean the one with the clock?

In Step 3 you
● do a questionnaire about friendship
● study nouns and adjectives describing personal qualities

so that you can
● express your opinion about friendships

1 Share your ideas
People

How many adjectives can you think of to describe people? Make two lists on the board.

Positive: friendly, kind, ...

Negative: selfish, ...

2 Reading

a **Reading skills**

Understanding new words

🔊 Listen, and read the questionnaire. Find the meaning of these words and expressions:

less   loyalty
get on well with
unkind   support
on my own   chatting

You can:
● guess the meaning from similar words in your language.
● guess the meaning from English words that you know.
● look at the rest of the sentence, and the sentences before and after it.
● use your dictionary.

b **Comprehension check**

Read the questionnaire again and choose your answers.

Then check your score in the key. Do you agree with the description?

Friends – how important are they?

❶ For me, friends are
  a more important than my family.
  b as important as my family.
  c less important than my family.

❷ In my opinion, the quality that's most important in a friend is
  a loyalty.
  b a good sense of humour.
  c honesty.

❸ I don't get on well with people who
  a are secretive.
  b are unkind.
  c try to control your life.

❹ My parents
  a know all my friends really well.
  b know some of my friends, but not all of them.
  c haven't met many of my friends.

❺ My friends and I
  a agree about nearly everything.
  b sometimes have different opinions.
  c often have different opinions.

❻ I think most people want friends who
  a always support them.
  b give them good advice.
  c respect their opinions.

❼ At the weekend I enjoy
  a playing sport or going shopping with my friends.
  b doing different things each week.
  c spending time with my family or on my own.

❽ When I go to a party,
  a I usually spend most of the time chatting to my friends.
  b I talk to people I know, but I like making new friends too.
  c I always have a good time. It doesn't matter who is there.

c **What do you think?** Compare your results. Have you got the same opinions about friendship?

For me, a good friend is someone who always supports you.

3 Word work   *Nouns describing personal qualities*

a Look at the examples. Then complete the nouns with the right ending from the box.

Erica's a **loyal** friend. Her **loyalty** is very important to me.
Mark's an **independent** person. I admire his **independence**.
Sue's really **kind**. She believes that **kindness** is the most important quality of all.

-ty   -ence   -ness

	Adjective	Noun
1	loyal	*loyalty*
2	independent	independ......
3	kind	kind......
4	confident	confid......
5	honest	hones......
6	generous	generosi......
7	patient	pati......
8	selfish	selfish......
9	sensitive	sensitivi......
10	thoughtful	thoughtful......

b Put the ten nouns in order of importance to you.

c If you have time, work with a friend and compare your opinions.

> I put 'honesty', 'sensitivity' and 'loyalty' first.

> I don't agree. I put 'kindness' first, then ...

Writing guide   *Expressing an opinion*

- To express your personal opinion, you can say:

  In my opinion, ...
  For me, the most important thing is ...
  I think ... / I don't think ...

- If you want to give an example, use:

  For example, ...

- If you disagree with other opinions, you can say:

  Some people think that ... , but I don't agree. / I disagree.

4 Writing   *About friendship*

Use what you know

What sort of person are you? Are friendships important in your life? Write two paragraphs.

Paragraph 1
Describe what you're like.

I'm quite a sociable person. For example, ...

Paragraph 2
Describe the qualities that are important to you.

In my opinion, the most important qualities in a friendship are ...
I like people who ...
I don't get on well with people who ...

Extra exercises

1 Complete the sentences with words describing flats and houses.

1 We live in a small _____ of flats.
2 The _____ isn't working. We'll have to use the stairs.
3 Mum's office is on the ground _____ of the building.
4 We haven't got a _____ , so we park the car in the street.
5 Mr Burke's house has got a _____ at the back. He grows flowers and vegetables in it.
6 Our flat has got a _____ which overlooks the square. We often sit there on warm evenings.

2 Match 1–8 with a–h and make eight sentences.

1 I've got some relatives
2 Thomas Edison was the scientist
3 The Beatles recorded songs
4 Giraffes are animals
5 A microwave is a machine
6 There's a ferry
7 Vesuvius is the volcano
8 We met your friend

a who plays the violin.
b that cooks food quickly.
c which destroyed the city of Pompeii.
d who were born in Turkey.
e who invented the electric light.
f which come from Africa.
g that were popular all over the world.
h that goes from Venice to Corfu.

3 Make sentences. Use the present simple and *who, which* or *that.*

1 *Mr and Mrs Stein are our neighbours who live upstairs.*

1 Mr and Mrs Stein / be / our neighbours _____ live / upstairs
2 Donna / sing / in a band _____ play / reggae music
3 We usually / get / the bus _____ go / along Queen Street
4 I / not like / people _____ be / selfish
5 Eduardo / be / a painter _____ come / from Argentina
6 They / own / a restaurant _____ serve / Asian food

4 Complete the conversation. Use the present simple or the present continuous.

A: I can see Chris over there. He ¹_____ a suit and tie! (*wear*)
B: You ²_____ ! He always ³_____ jeans. (*joke / wear*)
A: No, look! It's true.
B: Oh yes, I remember now. He ⁴_____ his new job this morning. (*start*)
A: He doesn't look very happy! I ⁵_____ he's very comfortable in those clothes. (*not think*)
B: Ssh! He ⁶_____ at us. He ⁷_____ it when people ⁸_____ at him. (*look / not like / laugh*)

5 Complete the conversations.

1 What sort of milkshake would you like?
   a I've got a chocolate one.
   b It's chocolate.
   c I'd like a chocolate one, please.
2 Have you got any boots?
   a Yes, I've got some black ones.
   b Yes, he has.
   c No thanks. I've got one.
3 Do you know Mr Hunter?
   a I don't know.
   b Yes, she's the one who lives in King Street.
   c No, I don't.
4 Which is your bag?
   a The big.
   b Yes, it's mine.
   c The big one.
5 Dave is going out with Tracey.
   a No, he isn't going.
   b Is she the tall one with dark hair?
   c Which ones do you mean?

6 How do you say these sentences in your language?

1 What floor is your flat on?
2 It's on the ground floor.
3 It overlooks the park.
4 Do you get on well with your neighbours?
5 I need a new jacket. I'd like a dark blue one.
6 Beth and Andy are engaged.

Life and culture

Poem

Look at the photo. What do you think the poem is about?

Good hope

I believe
There is enough food
On this planet
For everyone.

I believe
That it is possible
For all people
To live in peace.

I believe
We can live
Without guns,
I believe everyone
is important.

I believe there are good
Christians
And good Muslims,
Good Jews
And good not sures.
I believe
There is good in everyone.
I believe in people.

If I did not believe
I would stop writing.

I know
Every day
Children cry for water,
And every day
Racists attack.
Still every day
Children play
With no care for colour.

So I believe **there is hope**
And I hope
That there are many believers
Believing
There is hope.
That is what I hope
And this is what I believe.
I believe in you,
Believe me.

Benjamin Zephaniah

ABOUT BENJAMIN ZEPHANIAH

Benjamin and his twin sister were born in Birmingham in 1958 but he spent much of his childhood in Jamaica. He didn't enjoy school, but he always loved writing poetry. He started to perform his poems in public at the age of 15. He wanted to take poetry everywhere and to everyone and he has succeeded. Audiences of all colours and all ages love him. He often writes poems which are funny but which have a serious message too.

Task

Read the poem and discuss these questions with the class.

1 What sort of problems does Benjamin Zephaniah talk about? Find at least three.

2 Is he optimistic about the future?

3 Do you agree or disagree with him?

Unit 2　**21**

Grammar check

1 Present simple and present continuous
Work it out for yourself

A Look at the picture and choose the right sentences.

1 Sam's *playing* chess.
2 Sam *doesn't play* football.
3 Sam *plays* football and chess.
4 Sam *isn't playing* football.

B Match sentences 1–4 with explanations a–d.

1 Sam plays football every Saturday.
2 People all over the world play football.
3 Sam's playing chess.
4 Sam wants to win the chess game.

a a verb we don't normally use in the continuous form
b an action that is in progress now
c a present habit, a regular activity
d a fact that is generally true

Check that you can

● understand the difference between the present continuous and the present simple.

Match the questions and answers.

1 d

1 What do you do?
2 Do you know Tanya?
3 Is Jack at the sports centre?
4 What are you doing?
5 Can I use Dad's computer?
6 Is Leo interested in sport?
7 Does Paul need his old computer?
8 Are you doing your homework?

a Yes, he isn't using it.
b No, he doesn't use it.
c No, I don't want to do it now.
d I'm a waiter.
e I'm trying to do my maths homework.
f Yes, I see her at my judo class.
g Yes, he's playing tennis.
h Yes, he plays tennis.

2 Verbs + prepositions in *Wh-* questions
Work it out for yourself

Read the explanation. Then make a question for each picture. Use *look for, talk about, listen to*.

With a verb + preposition, we keep the preposition after the verb in *Wh-* questions.

1 A: What .... ?
   B: She's looking ....

2 A: What .... ?
   B: They're talking
   ....

3 A: What .... ?
   B: He's listening
   ....

Now complete the answers.

Check that you can

● make questions with a verb + preposition.

Put the words in the right order and make questions.

1 Who are you talking to?

1 A: I'm on the phone.
   B: to / you / who / talking / are ?
2 A: to / writing / who / you / are ?
   B: My friend in Canada.
3 A: I had a conversation with your brother last night.
   B: you / talk / what / about / did ?
4 A: you / are / for / waiting / what ?
   B: My pizza. It's nearly ready.
5 A: My friend's name is Václav.
   B: come / does / from / where / he ?
6 A: looking / you / are / at / what ?
   B: That red Ferrari.

3 Relative clauses
Work it out for yourself

Read the examples, then complete the explanation.

*I've got **a friend who/that** lives on a boat.*

*He's **the man who/that** owns the pizzeria.*

*A 'dotcom' is **a company that/which** sells things on the Internet.*

*This is **an insect that/which** exists only in Britain.*

We use *who* and sometimes .... to describe people. We use *that* or .... to describe things and animals.

Check that you can

● use relative pronouns to describe people and things.

Match 1–6 with a–f and make sentences using the relative pronoun.

1e Alfred Hitchcock was a film director who made horror films.

1 Alfred Hitchcock was a film director. (*who*)
2 Madonna is a singer. (*who*)
3 *Enormous* is an adjective. (*which*)
4 I know a good shop. (*that*)
5 I've got an uncle. (*who*)
6 My grandfather had a parrot. (*that*)

a He owns a restaurant in Manchester.
b It means 'very big'.
c It could say nearly fifty words.
d She's famous all over the world.
e He made horror films.
f It sells cheap DVDs.

4 one/ones
Work it out for yourself

A Look at the pictures and read the two dialogues. What do *one* and *ones* refer to?

BOY: *I know those girls.*
GIRL: *Which **ones**?*
BOY: ***The ones** at the front of the queue. **The one** with blond hair is in my class.*

BOY: *I'd like three pens – **a red one** and **two green ones**.*
WOMAN: ***The red one** is €2 and **the green ones** are €1.20 each.*

B Complete the explanations.

1 We use *one/ones* when we don't need to repeat the names of things and ....
2 We must use .... or .... after *a/the* + adjective. We say 'a red ....'. (**Not** 'a red'.)

Check that you can

● use *one/ones*.

Rewrite the dialogues in a different way without changing the meaning. Use *one/ones*.

1 A: Shall we sit at that table?
*   B: The one near the door?*
*   A: No, ...*

1 A: Shall we sit at that table?
   B: The table near the door?
   A: No, the table by the window.
2 A: Do you know those boys?
   B: Which boys?
   A: The boys who are chatting to Tom.
3 A: I'm staying at the hotel in Mill Street.
   B: Do you mean the new hotel, the hotel that overlooks the park?
4 A: What sort of headphones are you looking for?
   B: I want some cheap headphones. How much are the silver headphones over there?

Vocabulary and expressions

Verbs + prepositions
(to) argue about
(to) come from
(to) listen to
(to) look at
(to) look for
(to) talk about
(to) talk to
(to) think about
(to) wait for

Postcards
African
full moon
halfway
headphones
It sounds (funny)
low
nice and warm
right now
sunset
tour (n.)
(to) wonder

Words with *some/every*
everyone
everything
everywhere
someone
something
somewhere

Flats and houses
at the back
balcony
block of flats
first floor
garage
garden
ground floor
lift
(to) overlook
(to) own
stairs
What floor is it on?

Asking for clarification
Are they the ones with … ?
Do you mean the one with … ?
Was he the one who … ?
Which one do you mean?

Friendship
(to) chat
(to) control
(to) get on well with
less
mostly
quality
(to) respect
(to) rule
secretive
sense of humour
sociable
(to) support

Describing personality
confident – confidence
generous – generosity
honest – honesty
independent – independence
kind – kindness
loyal – loyalty
patient – patience
selfish – selfishness
sensitive – sensitivity
thoughtful – thoughtfulness

Study skills 1 Spelling

Look at the three groups of words, then complete the sentences below.

-s, -sh, -ch, -x + -s
bus > bus**es**
glass > glass**es**
crash > crash**es**
branch > branch**es**
box > box**es**

Verb + *-ing/-ed*	
live > liv**ing**	travel > travel**ling**
liv**ed**	travel**led**
move > mov**ing**	drop > drop**ping**
mov**ed**	drop**ped**

Consonant + *-y + -s*	Consonant + *-y + -ed*
a family > two famil**ies**	carry > carr**ied**
I carry > he carr**ies**	tidy > tid**ied**

1 Sara loves going abroad but she always .... (*miss*) her family.
2 Danny usually .... (*catch*) the number 44 bus to school.
3 Which .... (*quality*) are important to you in a friendship?
4 Our flat has got two .... (*balcony*) – one outside the living room and one outside the bedroom.
5 Nadia and Clare are .... (*argue*) about something. They're both very angry.
6 It's 8.15 and Danny is late. He's .... (*run*) to the bus stop.
7 Tom telephoned Matt last night and they .... (*chat*) about school.
8 Jamie .... (*marry*) Helen in 2004.

How's it going?

- ## Your rating

Look again at pages 22 and 23. For each section decide on your rating:
Good ✓ ✓ ✓   Not bad ✓ ✓   I can't remember much ✓

- ## Vocabulary

Choose at least three words from the Vocabulary list. Then work with a friend and ask *What does … mean? How do you spell it?*

- ## Test a friend

Look again at Units 1 and 2. Think of at least two questions, then ask a friend.

Who was Humphrey Bogart?   What does Danny do on Saturdays?

- ## Correcting mistakes

Can you correct these mistakes? In some sentences, there is more than one mistake.

1 I go to the cinema with Tom tomorrow.
   I'm going to the cinema with Tom tomorrow.
2 I know a girl which live in that block of flats.
3 Albert Einstein is born in 1879.
4 There's Emily. Who she waiting?
5 Do you want a large bottle or a small?

- ## Your Workbook

Complete the Learning Diaries for Units 1 and 2.

Coursework 1 — Our school magazine

Luke and Clare help to write a magazine for students at their school, Greenside Community College. It's called *Pulse* and it comes out twice a term. Here's a page from this month's edition.

Read the 'Who's who?' article from *Pulse*. Then make a magazine page about some of the people at your school.

Who's who at Greenside?

Find out more about the people who work at Greenside Community College.

Perhaps you're reading this article in the canteen, while you're eating your lunch. This month we'd like to introduce you to the person who does all the cooking. His name's **Del Stanley**. Del trained to be a chef in London and he came to Greenside College two years ago. He says 'I like using fresh, local food if I can. It isn't always easy to find things that everyone likes – teenagers are very unadventurous when they choose their meals!'

A lot of people say that our caretaker **Jeff Chapple** is the most important person in the school. He's the one who mends the heating when it stops working, locks the school at the end of the day and makes sure that the buildings are clean and safe. He told us, 'This certainly isn't a nine-to-five job. You have to start early in the morning, and work in the evening and at weekends too.' When he's got some free time, Jeff's an expert snooker player, and he's got a black belt in judo!

Mónica Gómez is our new language teaching assistant. She comes from La Coruña in northwest Spain. She's going to spend a year here. She's interested in learning languages, of course, and she also likes cycling and dancing. Have you tried her fantastic dance classes? They're every Thursday at 5.30 in the gym. At the moment, she's teaching her students salsa. Mónica says she likes Liverpool but she finds the local accent very difficult to understand. So, when you chat to her, remember to speak clearly!

Module 2

New horizons

In Module 2 Steps 1 and 2 you study

Grammar
- Past continuous and past simple
- *used to*
- *must/mustn't, have to/don't have to*
- Comparative adjectives
- Passive: present simple and past simple

Vocabulary
- Fears and fantasies
- Travelling by road

Expressions
- Expressing surprise
- Making travel arrangements

so that you can
- Describe events in the past
- Talk about coincidences
- Show interest and surprise
- Describe things that you imagine and worry about
- Describe things that happened in the past but don't happen now
- Talk about journeys and different forms of transport
- Book a trip
- Say when and where things are/were done

In Step 3 you ...

read
- An article about dreams
- An account of a journey around the world

study
- Link words
- Prepositions of movement
- Identifying the topic of a text
- Scanning a text for information

so that you can
- Write a description of a dream
- Write a journal about a journey

Life and culture

Haunted Britain
Journey into slavery

Coursework 2

Part 2 In conversation with Grace Lawson
You talk to an old person in your neighbourhood and write a short interview.

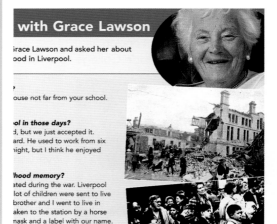

with Grace Lawson

Grace Lawson and asked her about
...ood in Liverpool.

...ouse not far from your school.

...ol in those days?
...d, but we just accepted it.
...ard. He used to work from six
...night, but I think he enjoyed

...hood memory?
...ated during the war. Liverpool
...lot of children were sent to live
...brother and I went to live in
...aken to the station by a horse
...nask and a label with our name.

What's it about?

What can you say about the pictures?

Now match the pictures with sentences 1–5.

1 There's a flight every day, but you have to change in Milan.
2 I used to jump into bed really quickly.
3 The pan caught fire when I was cooking the chips.
4 He saw the Great Wall of China.
5 Harley-Davidsons are known and loved by thousands of riders.

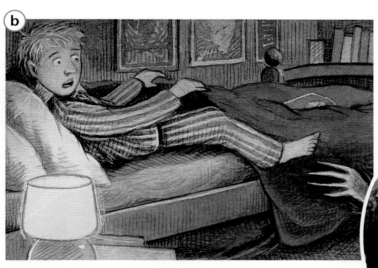

3 All in the mind

In Step 1 you study	so that you can
• past continuous and past simple	• describe events in the past
• expressing surprise	• talk about coincidences

1 Share your ideas

Do you know any twins? Would you like to have a twin brother or sister? People say that twins are often telepathic. Do you think that's possible?

> My cousins are twins. I don't know if they're telepathic!

2 Presentation *While I was playing baseball ...*

a What can you say about the pictures?

b 🎧 Close your book and listen to the conversation. How many strange coincidences does Toby describe?

Toby and Chris Porter are twins. Clare is asking Toby about being a twin.

CLARE: They say that twins are often telepathic. Is that true?

TOBY: Yes, I think it's true. I always know when Chris is in trouble.

CLARE: Really?

TOBY: Yes, and it's the same for him. For example, I remember one day when we were about eight. I was playing baseball in the garden with some friends. Chris wasn't playing. He was watching TV inside. Anyway, I was looking at my watch when the ball hit me in the face. Then Chris ran out of the house. He was crying and his nose was bleeding.

CLARE: That's strange! What a coincidence!

TOBY: Things like that happen all the time. Last week, while Dad and I were driving home, I smelt smoke. Dad stopped the car, and everything seemed fine. But when we stopped, I suddenly thought about Chris. So I rang him. He said, 'I can't talk now. The house is full of smoke! The pan caught fire when I was cooking some chips.'

CLARE: You're joking! How weird!

c 🎧 Listen again and follow in your book. Then ask and answer these questions.

1 What was Toby doing when the ball hit him?
2 What was Chris doing?
3 Why did Chris run out of the house?
4 What happened while Toby and his dad were driving home?
5 What did Toby's dad do?
6 When did Toby ring Chris?
7 When did the pan catch fire?

3 Key grammar *Past continuous and past simple*

Look at the examples and complete the explanations.

> Toby **was playing** baseball when the ball **hit** him.
> *or* When Toby **was playing** baseball, the ball **hit** him.
> While they **were driving** home, Toby **smelt** smoke.
>
> *In these sentences, one action was in progress when another action interrupted it.*
> *We can use* when *with the past* _____ *or the past continuous.*
> *We normally use* while *with the past* _____ .

G ▸ 8a

4 Practice

a Make complete sentences. Use the past simple and past continuous.

1 We were cooking dinner when Ben arrived.

1 We / cook dinner / when / Ben / arrive
2 When / I / get ready for school / my toast / catch fire
3 Danny's mum / meet her husband / when / she / visit Liverpool
4 While / Toby / wait for the bus / Chris / ring him
5 Andy / see an accident / when / he / go home
6 While / I / walk to school / I / drop my mobile

b Test a friend Say the first part of a sentence beginning *While I was ...ing ...* . Can your friend complete it?

(While I was walking to school, ...)

(... I found some money on the pavement.)

5 Key expressions *Expressing surprise*

Really?   That's strange!   How weird!
What a coincidence!   You're joking!

Make five dialogues. For each sentence, choose a response. Use each expression once.

(We've just won the lottery!)

(You're joking!)

1 We've just won the lottery!
2 My uncle and his wife were both born at midnight on 1st January.
3 I know Nicole Kidman.
4 My gran talks to the trees.
5 Toby says he can see into the future.

6 Listening and speaking
What a coincidence!

a ▭ Dave, Karen and Steve are talking about coincidences. Listen and match the names with the pictures.

5 Wingfield Street
Clapham
London SW4 7AD
UK

b ▭ Listen again, then ask and answer the questions.

1 Who did Dave meet while he was on holiday?
2 Why did he start talking to her?
3 What was Karen thinking about when she went into the shop?
4 Why was she so surprised?
5 Where was Steve going?
6 Steve and the person next to him had three things in common. What were they?

7 Writing and speaking
A strange coincidence

Use what you know

Write about another coincidence, then tell a friend about it.

I was travelling on a ... to ... when a girl/boy came and sat next to me. We started talking and we found out that ...

Listen to your friend's story and give your reaction.

In Step 2 you study	so that you can
● words describing fears and fantasies	● describe things that you imagine and worry about
● *used to*	● describe things that happened in the past but don't happen now

1 Key vocabulary *Fears and fantasies*

a ⏱ Match 1–8 with a–h. You've got three minutes!

1 Snakes don't **frighten** me but
2 I **feel nervous** when
3 My friend Jess **worries about**
4 I sometimes **have nightmares** if I
5 I don't know many people who **believe in**
6 Sometimes I **pretend** I'm OK
7 At night we often **dream about** things that
8 My little brother **makes up** stories

a ghosts.
b watch a horror film.
c happened during the day.
d everything – friends, clothes and school work!
e when I don't really feel OK.
f a lot of people hate them.
g about a monster called Durk.
h I have to speak in front of the class.

🔊 Listen and check.

b What about you? Choose at least three verbs or expressions from 1a and make more sentences.

> I sometimes pretend I'm older than 16.

> **Try this!**
> Make a list of things that frighten people.
> *thunderstorms, ...*

Luke
When we were little, my friend and I used to pretend there were dragons in our garden. We used to make 'dragon food' for them. And we didn't use to go behind the garage, because that was where the dragons used to sleep.

Nadia
My sister used to have an imaginary friend called Benley Hoofer. He lived in a tree outside her window and she used to have long conversations with him. Then, one day, when she was about six, Benley left. He went to Poland!

Danny
When I was a kid, I didn't use to believe in ghosts or monsters, but at night I used to think there was a weird little man under my bed. I used to jump into bed really quickly, so that he couldn't grab my feet!

2 Presentation
They used to believe in dragons

a 🔊 Listen to Luke, Nadia and Danny and follow in your book. Are they talking about:

1 things they believe in now?
2 things that happened recently?
3 things that happened in the past?

b Read the texts again, then answer the questions.

1 Does Luke believe in dragons now?
2 What did Luke and his friend use to do for the dragons?
3 Did Nadia's sister really have a friend called Benley?
4 What did she use to do?
5 Did Danny use to believe in ghosts?
6 Why didn't he like getting into bed?

4 Practice

a Complete the sentences with *used to / didn't use to* + one of these verbs.

> stay   believe   laugh   like   pretend
> have   worry

1 Clare ...*used to believe*... in Father Christmas. She was quite upset when she found out he didn't really exist.
2 Nadia .... maths, but she's very good at it now.
3 Danny .... a lot of nightmares when he was younger.
4 Toby .... about his school work, but now he gets nervous before exams.
5 I .... at my grandparents' house every summer. It was great.
6 Chris .... that he was a horse. We all .... at him!

b **What about you?** Make true sentences about yourself.

When I was younger, I used to / didn't use to:
– walk in my sleep.   – be frightened of the dark.
– have an imaginary friend.   – believe in vampires.

If you have time, make more true sentences.

5 Key pronunciation /j/

[recorder icon] Listen and repeat the words. Find the odd one out each time.

1 used to   you   juice   USA
2 Europe   usually   young   joke

[recorder icon] Now listen and practise this sentence.

Did you use to like your yellow uniform?

3 Key grammar used to

Look at the examples and complete the explanations.

> Nadia's sister **used to have** an imaginary friend.
> I **didn't use to believe** in ghosts.
>
> **Did** they **use to make up** stories?
> Yes, they **did**. / No, they **didn't**.
>
> *We use* used to *+ verb to talk about a regular activity or a situation in the past that doesn't happen now.*
> *The negative of* used to *is* ....
> *We make questions with* .... *+ subject + use to.*

[G icon] ➤ 9

6 Speaking When I was younger

Use what you know

Work with a friend and describe what you were like when you were younger. Find at least one thing which was the same for you and your friend, and one thing which was different. Then tell the class.

We both used to make up stories.

Maria used to pretend she was Batman, but I never used to do that.

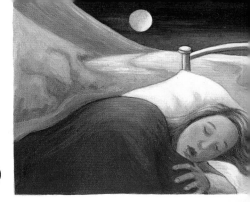

STEP 3

In Step 3 you
- read an article about dreams
- study link words

so that you can
- write a description of a dream

1 **Share your ideas** *Dreams*

Do you remember your dreams when you wake up? Do you often dream about the same things? Do you think dreams ever come true?

> I sometimes dream about school.

2 **Reading**

a Read the magazine article. Why is the dream in the article unusual?

THE IMPORTANCE OF DREAMS

1 All humans dream, and we know that animals and birds dream too. Dreaming helps our brains to work properly.

2 If you have eight hours' sleep a night, you probably dream for at least two hours. At first, you go slowly into a deep sleep without dreaming. Later, your sleep becomes lighter again, and then you begin to dream. Your heartbeat and your breathing become faster and your mind is very active.

3 Dreams can tell us a lot about our feelings, our hopes and fears – but they aren't always easy to understand. Some experts believe there are common 'dream images' that everyone shares. For example:

* a house is an image of yourself.
* a road means your journey through life.
* flying means freedom.
* falling means you're losing confidence or feeling out of control.
* water is a symbol of our emotions.

4 The ancient Greeks and Romans used to believe that dreams were messages from the gods – messages that told people about the future. Today, some people still think that dreams can predict the future.

Here's one famous example.

5 *President Abraham Lincoln had a dream in March 1865. In his dream, he was lying in bed when he heard people crying. He got up and, as he was walking through the corridors of the White House, the sound became louder. Finally, he arrived at the East Room. A dead man was lying inside. Soldiers were guarding him and a crowd of people were standing behind them. The dead man's face was covered. 'Who is dead in the White House?' Lincoln asked. 'The President,' a soldier answered. 'He was killed by an assassin.' Two weeks later, Lincoln was assassinated while he was sitting in a Washington theatre.*

b Comprehension check

🔊 Listen, and read the text again. Are these sentences true or false? Correct the false sentences.

1 Humans are the only living things that dream.
2 When we're asleep, we dream for about a quarter of the time.
3 Dreams about flying and falling aren't unusual.
4 In the past, people didn't use to think that dreams were important.
5 At the beginning of Lincoln's dream, he was walking through the White House.
6 While he was looking at the dead man, a lot of people came into the room.
7 Lincoln died in the White House in 1865.

c Reading skills *Identifying the topic*

Read the text again. Think about the topic of each paragraph, then match the five paragraphs with these headings.

Paragraph 1–c

a When you dream and how your body behaves
b An example of a dream that came true
c Dreaming – a normal part of life
d Some common dream images
e Beliefs about the importance of dreams

3 Word work *Link words*

a Look at the words in the box. Do you know what they mean?

when while as at first then later suddenly finally

b Choose the right words.

I had a nightmare last night. I was doing my homework in a strange room. [1](*Finally / At first*), I wasn't worried, because there were lots of other people there. But [2](*then / while*) they all disappeared. A few minutes [3](*when / later*), my science teacher appeared. Then, [4](*suddenly / while*) I was talking to her, her face [5](*when / suddenly*) changed and I felt really frightened. [6](*While / When*) I tried to run away, I couldn't move my legs properly. [7](*As / Later*) I was going up the stairs, she grabbed my foot. I was terrified! [8](*When / Finally,*) I woke up, but my heart was still beating really fast.

Writing guide *Describing a dream*

● Use adjectives to describe your dream.
I had a really weird/interesting/nice dream last night.

● Describe what you were doing at the beginning of the dream, and say what happened.
I was walking …   When/While …

● Use link words to join ideas.
Then/Later …   Suddenly, …

● Use adjectives to describe how you felt.
I was scared/lonely/happy/worried.
It was weird/awful/really frightening.

4 Writing *A strange dream*

Use what you know

Write about a dream. You can use ideas in the pictures on these pages.

Extra exercises

1 Complete the conversations. Use *one* word.

1 A: On Sunday I had a dream about scorpions. And the next day I found two scorpions in my room.
   B: _____ a coincidence!
2 A: There are about 6,800 languages in the world.
   B: _____ ? That's amazing.
3 A: The house was empty – but we could hear voices upstairs.
   B: How _____ !
4 A: Sam often has fish and chips for breakfast.
   B: You're _____ !
5 A: _____'s strange.
   B: What?
   A: I know I put my calculator in my bag, but now it isn't there.

2 Choose the right words and make complete sentences.

1 A funny thing (*happened / was happening*) this morning while I was coming to school.
2 We (*sat / were sitting*) in the garden when we suddenly saw a snake.
3 The owners weren't living in the building when it (*caught / was catching*) fire.
4 I had a cup of coffee when I (*got / was getting*) home.
5 While Kelly (*had / was having*) lunch, she made three phone calls.
6 When I dropped my glasses, they (*broke / were breaking*).
7 Someone (*hit / was hitting*) the side of our car while we were doing the shopping yesterday.
8 When the film ended, I (*turned off / was turning off*) the television.

3 Complete the conversations.

1 What was Liz doing when you rang her?
   a At half past eight.
   b She was listening to the radio.
   c She didn't want to talk to me.

2 I saw you outside the town hall this afternoon.
   a Yes, I was waiting for Martin.
   b What did you do there?
   c No, I didn't!

3 What did you do when you lost your bag?
   a I was travelling in Switzerland.
   b I went to the police station.
   c I was feeling worried.

4 Was it raining when you left home?
   a Yes, it did.
   b No, I didn't.
   c No, it wasn't.

5 When did Alex get off the train?
   a When it was going to London.
   b When it stopped at Bolton.
   c While he was walking to the station.

4 Choose the right words.

1 I don't often _____ nightmares.
   a have   b make   c dream
2 Most people feel _____ before an exam.
   a strange   b surprised   c nervous
3 When I was a child, I used to _____ I was Superman.
   a pretend   b make up
   c dream about
4 My parents _____ about me if I forget to ring them.
   a worry   b worries   c worried
5 Do you believe _____ vampires?
   a for   b in   c of
6 Mice don't _____ me.
   a frighten   b frightened
   c frightening
7 What sort of things do you dream _____ ?
   a along   b above   c about
8 My grandfather used to _____ up some incredible jokes.
   a invent   b make   c pretend

5 Complete the conversation. Use the right form of *used to*.

A: When I was little, we ¹_____ (*live*) in Prague.
B: ²_____ you _____ (*go*) to school there?
A: No, I didn't. I was very young. My grandmother ³_____ (*look*) after me while my parents were at work.
B: They say Prague's lovely. ⁴_____ you _____ (*walk*) round the city?
A: Yes, we did, but I ⁵_____ (*not enjoy*) it much. I ⁶_____ (*be*) frightened of the statues on the buildings! It sounds funny now. But things are different when you're young.

6 How do you say these sentences in your language?

1 How weird!
2 What a coincidence!
3 Chris is in trouble and he needs our help.
4 He smelt smoke.
5 The pan caught fire.
6 I'm frightened of snakes.

Extra reading

Haunted Britain

Do you believe in ghosts? Do you know about any haunted houses in your country?

Britain, it seems, is the most haunted country in the world and the Tourist Board has a list of more than 800 'haunted houses'.

'Glamis Castle has belonged to the same family, the Bowes-Lyons, since 1372. Queen Elizabeth's mother lived here. The Queen still stays at the castle from time to time. I visit it too. My name is Sampson and I used to work here. I was brought to Britain from West Africa with my mother in 1831. We were treated badly and I died when I was nine. Sometimes, at night, I sit on the stone seat outside the Queen's bedroom.'

A famous castle with many ghost stories is Glamis Castle in Scotland.

'My name is William Beckett. I lived in London in the 17th century. We were poor and my children were always hungry. One day I stole some food. I was caught and the judge, George Jeffreys, said I must die. Jeffreys used to be a regular customer at the Prospect of Whitby. He used to sit by the window and watch his victims on the gallows on the other side of the river. Sometimes we come back here. We can never forget him.'

People say that London is the most haunted city in the world. The Prospect of Whitby is one of its oldest riverside pubs.

'My name is Kate Penfound. My home is Penfound Manor. I died here on 26th April 1694, during the English Civil War. The war was between the Royalists, who supported the King, and the Roundheads, who were against the King. My father was a Royalist but I fell in love with John Trebarfoot, a Roundhead. One night, we were getting ready to run away together when my father found us. He killed us both. I come back here sometimes to look for John.'

Penfound Manor, in Cornwall, is one of the oldest houses in Britain.

ABOUT GHOSTS

In Britain, 29% of women and 25% of men say they believe in ghosts. One in eight people say they have seen one.

Task

Read the three stories, then answer the questions.

1 Was Sampson born at Glamis Castle?
2 Did he have a happy life there?
3 Where can you sometimes see him?
4 What was William Beckett's crime?
5 Do you think the judge was a kind man?
6 Why did Kate's father hate John Trebarfoot?
7 What did her father do when they were trying to escape?
8 Why does Kate go back to Penfound Manor?

4 Journeys

In Step 1 you study
- *must/mustn't, have to/don't have to*
- comparative adjectives
- making travel arrangements

so that you can
- talk about journeys
- book a trip to London

1 Share your ideas

Think of a journey that you would like to make. Where do you want to go, and why?

> I want to walk across the Pyrenees.

2 Presentation

You have to change in Milan

a 🔊 Look at the map and listen to the conversation. Does Danny say how much it costs to fly to Bangkok?

Danny's parents want to visit Thailand next month. They need to book their flight.

MRS GRAY: Barry, we really must book our flight soon.

MR GRAY: Yes, I know. We mustn't forget to go to the travel agent on Saturday.

DANNY: You don't have to go to a travel agent. Do it on the Internet! It's easier. Let's see ... There's a flight from Liverpool to Bangkok every day, but you have to change in Milan.

MRS GRAY: So there isn't a direct flight?

DANNY: You can get a direct flight from Heathrow. But it's more expensive.

MR GRAY: How far is it from here to Heathrow?

MRS GRAY: About 200 miles, I think.

MR GRAY: So how long does it take to get there?

DANNY: Hang on a minute ... Here we are. The train takes four hours. It's cheaper if you go by coach, but it takes longer.

MRS GRAY: Let's get a flight from Liverpool, then.

MR GRAY: OK. Shall we book it now? What do we have to do?

DANNY: You have to pay by credit card. Have you got your number?

b 🔊 Listen again and follow in your book. Are these sentences true or false? Correct the false sentences.

1. Mrs Gray wants to book their flight soon.
2. You can't book a flight on the Internet. You have to go to a travel agent.
3. There's a direct flight from Liverpool to Bangkok. You don't have to change.
4. Flights from Heathrow are cheaper than flights from Liverpool.
5. The train to Heathrow is quicker than the coach.
6. You need a credit card to book a flight on the Internet.

3 Key grammar must/mustn't, have to/don't have to

Look at the examples and complete the explanations with *mustn't, have to* or *don't have to*.

We **must** book our flight soon.
You **have to** change in Milan.

Must + verb and _____ + verb describe obligations. They both mean that something is necessary.

You **mustn't** lose your credit card!
You **don't have to** go to a travel agent.

Mustn't *and* don't have to *have different meanings.*
We use _____ *to give orders, and to describe obligations. There isn't a choice.*
We use _____ *to say that something isn't necessary. There is a choice.*

 G ➔ 16, 17

---

4 Practice

a Match 1–6 with a–f and make complete sentences.

1e The coach leaves at eight. We mustn't be late.

1 The coach leaves at eight. We mustn't
2 The flight from Heathrow is better because
3 If you want to go abroad, you must
4 Put your credit card in your bag. You
5 We don't have to take
6 When you go into a temple, you have

a have a passport.
b to speak quietly.
c you don't have to change.
d a map. We can buy one in Thailand.
e be late.
f mustn't lose it.

Remember!

Comparative adjectives
cheap > cheap**er**
easy > eas**ier**
expensive > **more** expensive
good > **better**   bad > **worse**

---

b Complete the sentences with comparative adjectives.

1 It's a lot _quicker_ (*quick*) if you go by train.
2 It's _____ (*easy*) if you get a direct flight.
3 The Bay Hotel is _____ (*expensive*) but it's _____ (*comfortable*).
4 I like travelling by train but flying is _____ (*exciting*).
5 Can I take your rucksack? It's _____ (*big*) than mine.
6 Why don't you go to Egypt? It's _____ (*near*) than Thailand.

---

5 Key expressions *Making travel arrangements*

a Complete the conversation with these expressions.

How long does it take?   It takes …
How far is it …?   I'd like to book …
When do you want to leave?   How can I get to …?

A: ¹_____ a flight to London, please.
B: ²_____
A: On the twenty-first of March.
B: There's a flight at 11.30, and one at three o'clock.
A: ³_____
B: ⁴_____ two and a half hours.
A: ⁵_____ the airport from here?
B: You can get a coach, or you can go by train.
A: ⁶_____ from the city centre?
B: About thirty kilometres.

b 🔊 Listen and check, then practise the conversation with a friend.

---

6 Key pronunciation *Stress in sentences*

🔊 Listen and repeat the sentences. Practise the stress.

1 How <u>long</u> does it <u>take</u>?
2 How <u>far</u> is it?
3 <u>How</u> can I get to the <u>airport</u>?

---

7 Writing and speaking *A trip to London*

Use what you know

Imagine you're at a travel agent's. You're booking a flight to London from your home.

In pairs, write a conversation like the one in Exercise 5, then act it. Add more details if you want to.

In Step 2 you study
- words for travelling by road
- present simple passive and past simple passive

so that you can
- talk about different forms of transport
- say when and where things are/were done

1 Key vocabulary *On the road*

a ⏱ Match the words with the pictures. You've got two minutes!

helmet   lorry   motorbike
petrol station   roundabout   scooter
speed limit   traffic lights   wheel

🔊 Listen and check.

b Test a friend Choose one of the words from 1a and make an anagram. Can your friend find the word?

BOTURUNODA

Try this!
Find the names of eight forms of transport.
NALEP   PISH   RAC   REFYR
CHOCA   UBS   RATIN   TABO

------

2 Presentation *They're loved by thousands!*

a 🔊 Listen to Andy and follow in your book. Why was 2003 an important year for Harley-Davidson fans?

I'm Andy. I ride a Harley-Davidson Sportster 883.

Harley-Davidsons are known and loved by thousands of riders. They're owned by many well-known stars. They're used by the police here in Britain, and in Germany too. Harley-Davidson helmets, jackets, boots, gloves and T-shirts are worn by fans all over the world.

The Harley-Davidson motorbike was designed and created in 1903 by 21-year-old William Harley and Arthur Davidson, aged 20. The first two bikes were produced in their garden in Milwaukee, Wisconsin, in the USA. They produced two more in 1904, and the following year their first factory was built. In 1908, the Harley-Davidson company was formed and its name soon became famous.

In August 2003, a huge birthday party was held in Milwaukee and more than 500,000 fans met to celebrate!

b 🔊 Read the text again. Then read these sentences. How do we know they are true? Find information in the text.

1 They're known and loved by thousands of riders.

1   Harley-Davidson motorbikes are very popular.
2   A lot of famous people have got one.
3   The British and German police use them.
4   The first two bikes weren't made in a factory.
5   In 1905 Harley and his partner built a factory.
6   Thousands of people were invited to the 100th birthday party.

3 Key grammar *The passive*

Complete the examples and read the explanations.

Harley-Davidsons **are known** all over the world.
The first bikes _____ **built** in 1903.

We form the passive with subject + the verb be + *past participle* (known, built).
We usually use the passive when the action is more important than the person or thing that does it.

They **were created** _____ William Harley and Arthur Davidson.

We use by *after the passive when we say who does the action.*

G ➤ *20a-b*

4 Practice

a Complete the sentences with these past participles.

> grown   made   used   played   spent   found

1 Most of the world's tigers are _____ in India.
2 The first jeans were _____ by Levi Strauss in 1873.
3 Olives are _____ in Spain and Greece.
4 The first football match was _____ in Cambridge in 1846.
5 Millions of pounds are _____ on fast food every year.
6 Dogs are often _____ to help the police.

b Complete the text. Use the present passive or past passive form of the verbs.

The first high-speed trains ¹_____ (*design*) in Japan in the 1950s. The first train line ²_____ (*open*) in 1964 and passengers ³_____ (*take*) from Tokyo to Osaka at 200 km an hour. Now there are trains that can travel at over 300 km an hour. The Japanese name for these trains is *Shinkansen*, but in English they ⁴_____ often _____ (*call*) 'bullet trains' because of their speed and shape.

High-speed trains ⁵_____ (*not introduce*) in Europe until the 1980s but now many countries have them. Today, these fast trains ⁶_____ (*use*) by more and more people and they are much better for the environment than planes.

5 Listening *Song*

a How do you say these words in your language?

> across   thunder   clouds   desert   miles
> hours   highway

b [cassette] Listen to the song. Do you think the singer is travelling:

a on a road?   b in a plane?   c in a boat?

c [cassette] Listen again and complete the lines from the song. Use the words in 5a.

1 Somewhere across the _____
2 Sometime in the early _____
3 On the open _____
4 Racing _____ the desert
5 At a hundred _____ an hour
6 Through the _____ and _____

6 Writing and speaking
Where was it made?

Use what you know

Think of an example for at least two of these topics. Describe them using the passive.

a form of transport   a well-known place
a type of food   something that you wear
a film   a song

The first car was produced in Germany.
My trousers are made of cotton.

In Step 3 you
- read about a journey round the world
- study prepositions of movement

so that you can
- write a journal about a journey

A very long bike ride

1 When Richard Gregg left the UK on a cycling trip, he planned to spend two or three years abroad. But, in the end, his trip lasted 14 years. 'There was so much to see.' he said. 'I decided to take my time.'

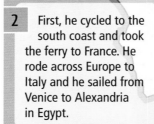

4 He rode through India, where he hurt his knee and had to go to hospital. When he was better, he crossed the Himalayas, travelled through Nepal and Tibet and then into China. He saw the Great Wall of China on his way to Beijing.

2 First, he cycled to the south coast and took the ferry to France. He rode across Europe to Italy and he sailed from Venice to Alexandria in Egypt.

3 He cycled along the banks of the River Nile to Aswan, and then he caught a train south across the desert, because there weren't any roads. While he was travelling through East Africa, he was chased by a rhino, but he arrived safely on the coast of Kenya. From there he flew to Pakistan.

1 Share your ideas
Travelling

How many different ways of travelling can you think of? Imagine you're going on a long journey. In your opinion, what's the best way of travelling, and why?

> I think cycling is good, because you see everything.

2 Reading

a Reading skills *Scanning*
🕐 Read the text quickly and find answers to these questions. Don't read every word. You've got three minutes!

1 How long did Richard's journey last?
2 How did he travel?
3 Where did he meet his wife?
4 Where did he get married?
5 Where did his journey finish?

b Match each photo with one of the paragraphs.

c Comprehension check
🔲 Listen, and read the text again. Then answer the questions.

1 How did Richard get to France?
2 Why didn't he cycle through the desert?
3 What dangerous experience did he have in Africa?
4 Why did he have to go to hospital?
5 What job did he get to earn more money?
6 Who travelled with him for part of his journey?
7 What happened in South America?

A

B

C

D

E

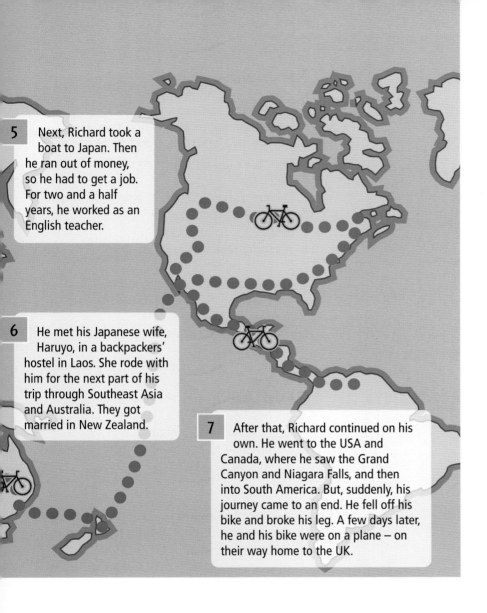

5 Next, Richard took a boat to Japan. Then he ran out of money, so he had to get a job. For two and a half years, he worked as an English teacher.

6 He met his Japanese wife, Haruyo, in a backpackers' hostel in Laos. She rode with him for the next part of his trip through Southeast Asia and Australia. They got married in New Zealand.

7 After that, Richard continued on his own. He went to the USA and Canada, where he saw the Grand Canyon and Niagara Falls, and then into South America. But, suddenly, his journey came to an end. He fell off his bike and broke his leg. A few days later, he and his bike were on a plane – on their way home to the UK.

3 Word work
Prepositions of movement

We often use prepositions with verbs such as *go, travel, ride, walk, run, cycle.*

He cycled **along** the banks of the Nile.
He rode **through** India.

Complete the texts with the prepositions in the box.

into	up	along	through
from	round	down	across

1 If you want to travel *from* England to France, you can sail _____ the English Channel on a ferry or you can go _____ the Channel Tunnel by train.

2 We rode our mountain bikes _____ the hill and had lunch at the top. Then we went _____ the other side of the hill and made a camp in the valley. In the afternoon we walked _____ a path that went _____ a small lake and then we went back to our camp. After that, we jumped _____ the lake for a swim.

Writing guide *Writing a journal*

- Use the past simple tense to describe events in the past:

  Paragraph 1
  I got up at …
  I left at … (time) to go to … (place)
  On the way to … , I saw/visited/bought …
  At lunch time I …

  Paragraph 2
  After lunch, I …
  It/The weather was …

- Use verbs + prepositions to describe journeys:

  I walked up … / rode across … / went into …

- Use link words, for example:

  before, after, then, after that.

4 Writing *Your journal*

Use what you know

Richard Gregg kept a journal of his journey round the world. Imagine you're doing the same. Choose one part of your trip and write about the day's events. Write one paragraph about the morning and one about the afternoon.

Where did you go?
Who and what did you see?
Did anything unusual happen?
How did you feel at the end of the day?

Extra exercises

1 Choose the right words.

1 The hotels are all more expensive in July _____ in June.
   a that   b than   c as

2 These T-shirts are nice, but the white ones are a lot
   _____ .
   a cheap   b more cheap   c cheaper

3 Is Dave's motorbike _____ fast as Andy's?
   a so   b as   c also

4 Why don't you buy a Japanese one? They're much _____ .
   a good   b cheap   c better

5 I'd like to go to Thailand because it's _____ beautiful than Tenerife.
   a more   b the more   c most

6 It's an awful song! It's a lot _____ than his earlier ones.
   a bad   b more bad   c worse

2 Complete the conversation. Choose from a–h.

A: ¹_____

B: About 1,200 kilometres.

A: ²_____

B: You can fly or you can get the train.

A: I'd like to go by plane. ³_____

B: No, you have to change at Amsterdam.

A: I see. ⁴_____

B: About four hours.

A: Is there a flight on the 18th of June?

B: Yes, there is. ⁵_____

A: Yes, please.

a Is there a direct flight?
b When do you want to travel?
c Would you like to travel to Lisbon?
d How can I get there?
e What do I have to do?
f Would you like to book it now?
g How far is it from here to Lisbon?
h So how long does the journey take?

3 Read the text. Put the letters in the right order and make words for travelling by road.

There was an accident in North Road this morning. I was coming out of the ¹*trelop intoast* on my ²*costore* when a black car went past. The ³*pedes itmil* is 50 km an hour, but the car was travelling a lot faster than that. When it got to the ⁴*bouraduton*, it didn't stop. A ⁵*trimokobe* was coming from the right and its front ⁶*hewel* was hit by the car. It was lucky that the rider was wearing a ⁷*methel*. He fell off his bike, but he wasn't hurt.

4 Complete the second sentence so that it means the same as the first one. Use *must, have to, mustn't, don't have to.*

1 It's necessary for drivers to stop at a red traffic light.
   Drivers *have to stop* at a red traffic light.

2 Don't touch that hot pan.
   You _____ that hot pan.

3 It's important that I find my keys.
   I _____ my keys.

4 You can book the flight now, but it isn't necessary.
   You _____ the flight now.

5 Don't use your mobile when the plane is landing.
   You _____ your mobile when the plane is landing.

6 I don't want to stay at home tonight, but it's necessary.
   I _____ at home tonight.

7 It's possible to pay by credit card, but you don't need to do it.
   You _____ by credit card.

5 Complete the sentences. Use the present simple passive or past simple passive form of the verbs.

1 A lot of cheese _____ in France. (*produce*)
2 The first car _____ by a German called Karl Benz. (*design*)
3 Magazines _____ in a newsagent's. (*sell*)
4 The first Harley-Davidson motorbike _____ in a factory. (*not make*)
5 In 2004 the Olympic Games _____ in Athens. (*hold*)
6 Bananas _____ in this country. (*not grow*)

6 How do you say these sentences in your language?

1 We must book our flight.
2 You don't have to go to a travel agent.
3 Is there a direct flight?
4 The journey takes seven hours.
5 How far is the airport from here?
6 A huge party was held in 2003.

Journey into slavery

Do you know anything about the African slave trade?

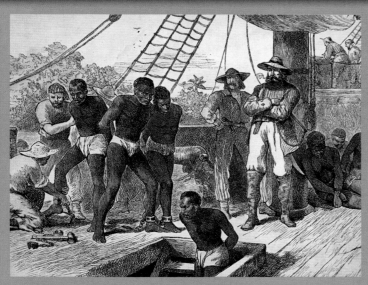

English slave traders took their ships from the ports of Liverpool and Bristol to the west coast of Africa, and then across the Atlantic.

Slavery has existed for thousands of years and it still exists in some parts of the world. But the worst period of slavery in modern history was from the 1500s to the 1880s. Millions of Africans were taken by the English, and also by the Spanish, Portuguese and French, to the new colonies in North and South America and the Caribbean.

Thousands of people died during the journey across the Atlantic because of the terrible conditions on the ships. Those who survived were sold at markets. Families were often separated for ever. The slaves worked on the plantations that grew tobacco, rice, sugar and cotton, and in the homes of the plantation owners.

ABOUT AFRICAN MUSIC

The music that the slaves took with them from Africa to America was the origin of many types of modern music: jazz, blues, rock and rap, for example.

Life was extremely hard and many slaves tried to escape. If they were caught, they were cruelly punished.

One of the first strong voices against slavery belonged to a slave called Olaudah Equiano. He wrote a book about their suffering. Later, another book – *Uncle Tom's Cabin* by Harriet Beecher Stowe – also helped to change public opinion. In 1787 the Abolition Society was formed in Britain, but twenty years passed before the British slave trade was stopped. Slavery continued in the USA for many years after that, mainly in the southern states.

In the northern states, the campaign to abolish slavery became stronger and from 1861 to 1865 there was a Civil War between the northern states and the southern states. The North won. Then all the slaves were freed but, in fact, they had fewer rights than white people. It was not until the 1960s that campaigners such as Martin Luther King began the Civil Rights movement, and finally all blacks were given equal rights in education, jobs and voting.

Task

Read the text, then answer the questions.

1 Where were the African slaves taken?
2 Why did many people die during the journey?
3 What happened when they arrived?
4 Why was it dangerous to try to escape?
5 How did Olaudah Equiano help to change public opinion?
6 Was slavery more common in the northern states or the southern states?
7 When did all American slaves finally become free?
8 Were whites and blacks equal after that?

Module 2 Review

Grammar check

1 Past simple and past continuous
Work it out for yourself

A Look at the pictures. Match the questions and answers.

1 *What **did** Jack **do** when he saw Miriam?*
2 *What **was** Jack **doing** when he saw Miriam?*

a *He **was going** to school when he **saw** her.*
b *He **fell** off his bike when he **saw** her.*

B Now match answers a and b with these explanations.

1 One action was in progress; another action interrupted it.
2 One action came **after** the other.

Check that you can

1.1 ● use the past simple and the past continuous.

Complete the sentences.

1 It __started__ (start) to rain while we __were playing__ (play) volleyball.
2 We .... (fall) asleep when we .... (watch) TV.
3 While we .... (stay) in London, we .... (take) a boat trip on the Thames.
4 Someone .... (steal) my bag while I .... (play) tennis.
5 A: Where .... (you/go) when you .... (have) the accident?
   B: I was going to the sports centre.

1.2 ● show that one action came after the other.

Complete the sentences.

1 I __burnt__ (burn) my finger when the pan __caught__ (catch) fire.
2 When I .... (phone) Sally, she .... (not answer).
3 When the ball .... (hit) Toby, he .... (start) to cry.
4 When Tim .... (hear) the joke, he .... (not laugh).
5 A: What .... (you/do) when you .... (lose) your passport?
   B: I went to the police station.

2 used to
Work it out for yourself

A Read the sentences and answer the questions.

THE PAST

NOW

*Debbie **used to** be a businesswoman in London.*
*She **didn't use to** be a farmer.*
***Did** she **use to** work outside? – No, she **didn't**.*
*She **used to** sit in an office all day.*

1 In her old job, did she usually work inside?
2 Does she work inside now?

B Complete the explanation. Choose the right words.

Used to + verb describes a regular activity in the *past / present*. The activity *happens / doesn't happen* now.

Check that you can

● talk about regular past activities.

Make sentences about the past using *used to / didn't use to*.

1 *I used to believe in ghosts.*

1 I don't believe in ghosts now.
2 I don't have nightmares now.
3 My sister listens to Mozart now.
4 I eat a lot of fish now.
5 My aunt's a teacher now.
6 They sell DVDs at the supermarket now.
7 I'm not scared of dogs now.
8 Ben doesn't worry about exams now.

3 must/mustn't, have to/don't have to

Work it out for yourself

A Look at the picture and complete the explanation.

I have to clean my room. I must find my maths book.

We use .... or .... to say that something is necessary.

B Match pictures A and B with sentences 1 and 2. Then complete the explanations with *mustn't* and *don't have to*.

(A) (B)

1 *You **don't have to** use your mobile.*
2 *You **mustn't** use your mobile.*

We use .... to express a necessary obligation.

We use .... to say that something isn't necessary.

Check that you can

● say what is an obligation and what isn't necessary.

Choose the right answer.

1 I (*mustn't / don't have to*) take sandwiches. I can eat at the café.
2 Hurry up! You (*mustn't / don't have to*) be late!
3 You (*must / mustn't*) wear a helmet if you want to ride on my motorbike.
4 You (*mustn't / don't have to*) go too fast. Remember the speed limit!
5 Paul's tired. He (*mustn't / has to*) get up at five o'clock every morning.
6 Jenny's lucky. She (*mustn't / doesn't have to*) work this weekend.

4 The passive

Work it out for yourself

Look at the pictures and read the sentences. Then answer the questions.

Active

1 *Sarah **locks** her front door every night.*

Passive

2 *The park gate **is locked** at ten o'clock every night.*

a Do we know who locks the front door?
b Do we know who locks the park gate?
c In which sentence (1 or 2) are we interested in the action and the person who does the action?
d In which sentence are we more interested in the action?

Check that you can

● use the present and past simple passive.

Complete the sentences. Use the present or past simple passive form of the verbs.

1 The stories aren't true. They _were made up_ (*make up*) by the writer.
2 The planet Pluto .... (*not discover*) until 1930.
3 In the 18th century, the castle .... (*guard*) by a hundred soldiers.
4 Bears .... (*not find*) in Britain now.
5 Today, 50% of plane tickets .... (*book*) on the Internet.
6 I .... (*chase*) by a dog on my way to school this morning.
7 Mario's scooter .... (*steal*) yesterday.
8 My dad's car .... (*hit*) by a lorry last night, but he .... (*not hurt*).

Vocabulary and expressions

Expressing surprise
How weird!
Really?
That's strange!
What a coincidence!
You're joking!

Fears and fantasies
(to) believe in
(to) dream about
(to) feel nervous
(to) frighten
(to) have nightmares
(to) make up
(to) pretend
(to) worry about

Dreams
active
breathing
(to) come true
corridor
(to) cover
deep
fear
freedom
god
(to) guard
heartbeat
image
mind
out of control
properly
soldier
symbol

Link words
as
at first
finally
later
suddenly
then
when
while

Making travel arrangements
How long does it take?
It takes …
How can I get to … ?
How far is it?
I'd like to book …
When do you want to leave?

On the road
helmet
lorry
motorbike
petrol station
roundabout
scooter
speed limit
traffic lights
wheel

Travelling
backpacker
bank (of a river)
bike ride
(to) chase
(to) fall off
in the end
(to) last
on his way to
(to) plan
(to) run out of
safely
valley

Prepositions of movement
across
along
down
from
into
round
through
up

Study skills 2 Guessing what words mean

When you're trying to understand a new word, it helps if you can see what part of speech it is. Is it a noun, a verb, an adjective, an adverb or a preposition?

⏱ In each of the following sentences, there is a 'nonsense word' in *italics*. Look at the nonsense word, work out the part of speech, then find a real word to complete the sentence. You've got five minutes!

1 Maria is a *scooper*. She works in a hospital. *noun doctor or nurse*
2 Everyone did the exercise *loply* so we finished it before the end of the lesson.
3 Tarik is sitting *ubit* his friend Salim.
4 Horror films don't *ribrac* me. In fact, I enjoy them.
5 It was a very *pensey* experience and Tom didn't sleep well that night.
6 Helen and her friends are *hottying* to speak Russian.
7 I want to make something to eat but there aren't any clean *cottles*.
8 I started to fall but Dave *garted* my hand so I was OK.

Work with a friend and compare your answers.

How's it going?

- **Your rating**

Look again at pages 44 and 45. For each section decide on your rating:
Good ✓ ✓ ✓   Not bad ✓ ✓   I can't remember much ✓

- **Vocabulary**

Look at the Vocabulary list and find at least three adjectives, two adverbs, and two words which can be verbs or nouns.

- **Test a friend**

Look again at Units 3 and 4. Think of at least two questions, then ask a friend.

> What does the word 'twin' mean?

> How did Mr and Mrs Gray book their holiday?

- **Correcting mistakes**

Can you correct these mistakes? In some sentences, there is more than one mistake.

1 ~~When we got to their house they eat their dinner.~~
2 ~~Debbie mustn't go to the school tomorrow. It's Saturday.~~
3 ~~Those flats are builded in the 1950s.~~
4 ~~They used live in Portugal but now they live in France.~~
5 ~~English is more easy that Chinese.~~

- **Your Workbook**

Complete the Learning Diaries for Units 3 and 4.

Coursework 2   *Our school magazine*

Read the interview in this month's edition of *Pulse*. Then talk to an old person in your community and ask them about their childhood. Write a short interview in English.

In conversation with Grace Lawson

This month we interviewed Grace Lawson and asked her about her memories of her childhood in Liverpool.

Were you born in Liverpool?
Yes, I was born in 1931, in a house not far from your school. It doesn't exist now.

What was life like in Liverpool in those days?
For most families, life was hard, but we just accepted it. My father worked in the shipyard. He used to work from six in the morning until seven at night, but I think he enjoyed his job.

What's your most vivid childhood memory?
The day when we were evacuated during the war. Liverpool was very badly bombed, so a lot of children were sent to live in the country. I was nine. My brother and I went to live in North Wales. Our bags were taken to the station by a horse and cart. We both had a gas mask and a label with our name. Everyone tried not to cry but I remember we were very frightened. Some of the children never saw their parents again.

What do you particularly remember about that time?
We lived on a farm and we used to help with the animals. I looked after the hens and I used to love collecting the eggs.

What was it like after the war?
At first, of course, there were huge celebrations – everyone danced in the streets in the city centre. But for us, life soon went back to normal – school, and homework!

Do you think children were happier when you were young?
Yes, I think they were. We didn't have computers or TVs. We played together all the time, often in the street. We didn't worry about all the things that young people worry about now. Life used to be more fun, it seems to me.

Module 3

Changes

In Module 3 Steps 1 and 2 you study

Grammar
- Present perfect with *just, yet, already*
- *been* and *gone*
- Present perfect and past simple
- *its*: possessive adjective
- Present perfect with *for* and *since*
- Present perfect with superlative adjective + *ever*
- Superlative adjectives
- *give* + direct and indirect object

Vocabulary
- Topics in the news
- Personal possessions

Expressions
- Offers and suggestions
- Time expressions

so that you can
- Describe recent events and give your news
- Talk about things people have and haven't done
- Offer to help and make suggestions
- Make a radio report
- Talk about things in the present that started in the past
- Give details about your background
- Talk about your favourite possessions
- Describe important things and events

In Step 3 you ...

read
- An article about a volcano
- An interview with someone who lives abroad

study
- *so ... that ...* and *such a/an ... that ...*
- *still, any more*
- Understanding the main idea of a text
- Skimming a text for the general idea

so that you can
- Write about recent events for a school newsletter
- Write a personal account

Life and culture

Non-stop news
New Zealand

Coursework 3

Part 3 Reviews
You write a review of a book, film or TV programme.

Reviews ★ ★ ★

If you want to know about the best books, films and TV prog from some of our readers.

Books

The Curious Incident of the Dog in the Night-Time by Mark Haddon is the best book I've read for a long time. I couldn't put it down! It's about a 15-year-old boy called

Films

I've seen *The Incredibles* three ti now and I love it! It's fast, excitin and very funny. At the beginning the film, the Parrs – Bob, Helen, Violet, Dash and Jack-Jack – lool

What's it about?

What can you say about the pictures?

Now match the pictures with sentences 1–5.

1 My relatives have lived in the USA for a long time.
2 My father gave it to me.
3 Have they finished its head yet?
4 Does Yellowstone Park get a lot of visitors?
5 How many medals has he won?

5 In the news

STEP 1

In Step 1 you study
- words for topics in the news
- present perfect (+ *just*)
- *been* and *gone*

so that you can
- describe recent events
- write an email giving your news

1 Key vocabulary *Topics in the news*

a ⏱ Match the topics with the sentences from the newspaper. You've got two minutes!

crime   the environment   famous people
health   politics   sport   war and peace
the weather

1. **Researchers have found that eating chocolate is good for you ...**

2. Tomorrow will be cool and cloudy ...

3. **A bridge was destroyed and three soldiers were injured ...**

4. **Stars from all over the world are in Hollywood this week ...**

5. **More than £2 million was stolen from a bank ...**

6. **Schoolchildren have planted a thousand trees ...**

7. **British athletes have won two gold medals ...**

8. World leaders are meeting in Beijing today ...

🔊 Listen and check.

b **What do you think?** Which topics are you interested in? Which ones do you think are the most important?

> I'm quite interested in politics.

2 Key pronunciation /s/ + consonant

🔊 Listen and repeat the words.

sport   stars   school   smoke   sleep

🔊 Now listen and practise this sentence.

Steve Small studies Spanish at school but he still speaks slowly.

3 Presentation *What's happened recently?*

a 🔊 Cover the text and listen to Danny's email. Which of these topics are mentioned?

Danny's neighbours   the weather
school   sport   Danny's family

Danny's writing to his friend Callum, who used to live at Mandela Court.

From: Danny
Subject: News

Hi Callum!

Sorry I haven't written recently. I've been busy because we've had four tests at school this week.

Everyone's fine here. Beth and Andy are getting married soon and Mum has bought me a suit for the wedding! Beth sends you her love. Dad and Mum aren't here at the moment. They've gone to Thailand on holiday.

What else has happened? Luke has just won a big maths competition – he's in the local paper this week. And Winston and Lorina have had another baby. They've called him Justin. There's a new leisure centre in Sydney Street. I've been there a few times and it's very good.

What about you? Has anything interesting happened recently?

The football has just started on TV so I'll say goodbye now.

Write soon.
Danny

b 🔊 Listen again and follow in your book. Then complete the sentences using words from Danny's email.

1 he's had four tests at school.

1. Danny has been busy this week because ...
2. Danny's parents aren't there because ...
3. Luke is in the paper this week because ...
4. ... and he's four days old now.
5. Danny likes the new leisure centre. He's ...
6. He wants to finish his email because ...

4 Key grammar   *Present perfect (+ just)*

Read the examples and complete the explanations.

> I **haven't written** recently.
> Lorina **has had** a baby.
> Mr and Mrs Gray **have gone** to Thailand.
>
> *We can use the present perfect to describe recent actions and events. We often use it to give a piece of news.*
> *We form the present perfect with* have/_____ *or* _____/
> hasn't + *past participle of the verb.*
>
> The football has **just** started.
>
> *We use the present perfect +* _____ *for something that happened a short time ago.*
>
> He's/She's/It's started. = He/She/It **has** started.

G ➔ 4

Remember!

The past participle of the verb go *can be* been *or* gone.
Danny **has been** to the leisure centre. =
He was there but now he has come back.
Mr and Mrs Gray **have gone** to Thailand. =
They are there now.

5 Practice

a Complete the sentences with the present perfect form of these verbs.

> buy   go   forget   have   start   try

1 I can't get any money. I *'ve forgotten* to bring my bank card.
2 I _____ to phone Clare but she isn't in.
3 Beth isn't here. She _____ to work.
4 Come and sit down! The film _____ .
5 Danny _____ a shower and now he's getting dressed.
6 Andy's walking home from the shops. He _____ a chicken and some vegetables.

b Describe the four faces and imagine what has just happened. Use *happy, upset, angry, frightened.*

> She's happy because her basketball team has just won.

Try this!

Find five past participles. What do the other words mean in your language?
FORGOTTEN   BEAN   MET   BEGUN
STARTER   FINISHED   PLANT   DONE

6 Speaking and listening
The latest news

a What can you say about the photos?

b 🔊 Listen to the news and match the news items with the photos.

c 🔊 Read the questions, then listen again and find the answers.

1 Why is the President of the World Bank in London?
2 Where were the bones found?
3 How much money has the national park received?
4 How many gold medals has André Fitz won?
5 What will the weather be like in Scotland tomorrow?

7 Writing   *Your news*

Use what you know

Write an email to a friend or relative telling them your news.

A new family has just moved into our street.

Invent some news if you want to.

My brother Billy has won a medal in the Olympics.

In Step 2 you study
- present perfect + *yet, already*
- present perfect and past simple
- offers and suggestions

so that you can
- talk about things people have and haven't done
- offer to help and make suggestions
- make a radio report

1 Share your ideas

a Look at the photo and read about the WEEE Man. What other things did Paul Bonomini use, do you think?

> I can see a washing machine.

b What do people do with electrical equipment when they don't want it any more?

2 Presentation *We haven't finished its head yet*

a  Listen to the interview and follow in your book. Have Paul and Martha got everything they need?

Beth works for a local radio station. She's interviewing two art students who are building their own WEEE Man. She's asking them about their progress.

BETH: How's it going? Have you finished it yet?

PAUL: No, not yet. We've already made most of the body and we've finished the neck. We used a tube from a vacuum cleaner for that. But we haven't finished its head yet.

MARTHA: We've made the eyes and the nose, but we've only made one of its ears. We need another satellite dish.

PAUL: And we haven't finished its mouth yet. We haven't got enough mice.

BETH: Mice?

PAUL: Yes – computer mice! For its teeth.

BETH: Oh, yes, of course. Have you been to the recycling centre?

MARTHA: Yes, we have. We've already been there several times. We went again yesterday.

BETH: Well, shall I ask the listeners if they can help? Why don't you give me a list of the things you need? I could read it on my next programme.

PAUL: That's a great idea. Thanks very much.

The WEEE Man, a sculpture by Paul Bonomini

The WEEE Man is seven metres tall and weighs three tonnes. It represents the amount of electrical equipment that the average person throws away in a lifetime – for example, fridges, microwaves, vacuum cleaners and phones.

b Read the conversation again. Then ask and answer the questions.

> Have Paul and Martha finished their project yet?

> No, they haven't.

1 Have Paul and Martha finished their project yet?
2 Have they finished the body yet?
3 Have they made the neck?
4 Have they finished its face yet?
5 Have they been to the recycling centre?

Remember!

The sculpture hasn't got all **its** teeth.
Its *is a possessive adjective.*
Be careful!
It's great. = **It is** …
It's been in the news. = **It has** been …

3 Key grammar *Present perfect + yet, already; present perfect and past simple*

Look at the examples and the explanations. How do you say the examples in your language?

Have you **finished** it **yet**?
We **haven't finished** its head **yet**.

We use yet *+ present perfect in questions and in negative sentences.*

They**'ve already made** its left ear.
They **made** it yesterday. They **used** a satellite dish.

We use the past simple after the present perfect if we say when something happened, or give more details.

G ➔ 3a-b, 4

4 Practice

a For each picture, make one sentence with *already* and one sentence with *yet*.

1 He's already started his science project. He hasn't finished it yet.

start / his science project
finish / it

take / their exams
have / their results

wash / the pans
tidy / the kitchen

eat / her lunch
finish / her coffee

b Complete the sentences using the present perfect or the past simple. Work with a friend and practise the conversation.

A: It's very nice here, isn't it?
B: Yes, it is. I ¹_____ (*already/eat*) here a couple of times. I ²_____ (*eat*) here last week.
A: Really? ³_____ (*you/come*) with Pete?
B: No, I ⁴_____ (*come*) with Dave.
A: Er … ⁵_____ (*you/see*) the film at the Odeon yet?
B: Yes, I have. I ⁶_____ (*see*) it on Saturday.
A: ⁷_____ (*you/go*) with Dave?
B: No, I ⁸_____ (*go*) with Emma.

5 Key expressions *Offers and suggestions*

Shall I ask the listeners?
I could read it on the radio.
Why don't you give me a list? / You could give me a list.

Choose at least three situations and make an offer or a suggestion. *Use Shall I/we … ?, Why don't we/you …?* or *I/You/We could … .*

1 Shall I do the washing up?

1 You're offering to help at home.
2 You're with some friends. Everyone is bored and it's raining.
3 You're at home with a friend. You're both hungry.
4 It's a friend's birthday soon and you want to do something special for her.
5 A friend is at your house/flat. It's late and he's just missed the last bus home.

6 Writing and speaking *A radio report*

Use what you know

Prepare the radio report about Paul and Martha. Say what they've already done and what they haven't done yet. Then read your report to a friend.

They haven't made … yet.
They've already …
Can you help? They need …

STEP 3

In Step 3 you
- read about a volcano
- study *so ... that ...* and *such a/an ... that ...*

so that you can
- write about recent events for a school newsletter

Places in the news

Yellowstone's hot secret

Visitors to America's world-famous Yellowstone Park have always been fascinated by its thousands of hot springs and geysers. But they have only just begun to understand what they're looking at. Every year, more than three million people walk over one of the largest active volcanoes in the world.

Yellowstone is a supervolcano. After the last big eruption 640,000 years ago, ash covered most parts of North America, and the Earth's climate changed. During the 'volcanic winter' that followed, clouds of dark ash hid the sun. It was so cold that many types of animals and plants died. The eruption made such a huge hole that we can only see it from the air. It is 85 km long and 45 km wide.

The volcano is still alive. Tests have shown that thousands of earthquakes happen every year at Yellowstone. They are usually so small that people can't feel them, but they are signs of volcanic activity. Recently, the number of earthquakes has increased and, in some parts of the park, the level of the ground has risen. The Yellowstone Volcanic Observatory is using sensitive new equipment to find out more about these movements.

Yellowstone has had three super eruptions in the last 2.1 million years. Most experts believe there is no immediate danger of another giant explosion, but it's impossible to be sure. Alan Stewart, a London scientist, says: 'There's going to be another super eruption somewhere on the planet. They've already happened in the past. They aren't going to stop happening because humans have appeared!'

1 Share your ideas
Following the news

How often do you read a newspaper or watch the news on TV? What's been in the news recently?

> I quite often watch the news on TV. This week ..... has been in the news.

2 Reading

a Read the text. Is it an article for:
- a scientists?
- b people on holiday?
- c people who are interested in the natural world?

b **Comprehension check**

Listen, and read the text again. Then answer these questions.

1 Does Yellowstone Park get a lot of visitors?
2 What amazing fact have people learnt recently?
3 When was the last super eruption at Yellowstone?
4 Why was it such an important event?
5 Why isn't it possible to see the hole from the ground?
6 Are there still earthquakes at Yellowstone today?
7 What has happened at Yellowstone recently?
8 Do most experts think that the volcano is going to erupt soon?

c **Reading skills** *Understanding the main idea*

1 What is the topic of the text?
- a famous places
- b a supervolcano
- c volcanoes

2 What do you think is the main idea? Read the beginning and end again, then choose the best answer.

It's about ...
- a what happens when there is a volcanic eruption.
- b an ancient volcano that isn't active now.
- c a huge volcano that is still active.

One World Magazine

3 Word work so … that …; such a/an … that …

Look at the examples.

The hole is **so huge that** we can only see it from the air.

It is **such a huge hole that** we can only see it from the air.

Join the sentences using *so* + adjective + *that* … or *such a/an* + adjective + noun + *that* … .

1 The traffic was so bad that it took two hours to get home.

1 The traffic was bad. It took two hours to get home.
2 I felt nervous. I couldn't eat.
3 It was a good film. We bought the DVD.
4 The test was difficult. Nearly everyone failed.
5 I had a horrible nightmare. I felt upset all morning.
6 It was a boring match. Danny fell asleep.
7 Mr and Mrs Gray had a good time in Thailand. They didn't want to go home.
8 The weather was cold last winter. A lot of birds died.

Writing guide *Writing a newsletter*

● For each event, say what has happened. Use the present perfect.

Class 10JC has been on a science trip.
Our school has won the National Volleyball Championship.

● Give more details. Use the past simple.

They went to the Science Museum in … last Wednesday.
It took place last Saturday. In the final, our team beat …

4 Writing *A school newsletter*

Use what you know

Think of things that have happened recently at your school. Write a description of at least one event for a school newsletter. You can use these ideas or think of your own.

– a class trip
– a school concert or social event
– sports news
– a student or teacher who has left or arrived
– a problem that the school has had

Extra exercises

1 Match the word groups 1–8 with the news topics a–h.

1 ocean, forest, pollution
2 medicine, doctor, illness
3 actor, pop star, president
4 hot, windy, sunny
5 prime minister, meeting, government
6 steal, kill, police
7 basketball, hockey, tennis
8 soldiers, fight, die

a the weather
b crime
c the environment
d sport
e war
f health
g famous people
h politics

2 Complete the sentences with *just, yet* or *already*.

1 The bread's still hot. Mum's _____ taken it out of the oven.
2 I don't want to watch that film. I've _____ seen it three times.
3 We haven't done the washing up _____ .
4 Don't tell that old joke again! Everyone's _____ heard it.
5 Has the meeting started _____ ?
6 A: Your hair's wet.
   B: Yes, I've _____ had a shower.

3 Read the text and choose the right word(s) for each space.

The school holidays have just ¹_____ and we're going away tomorrow. Mum ²_____ the plane tickets last week, and ³_____ already booked a taxi to take us to the airport. Everyone ⁴_____ worried last night because Dad ⁵_____ find his passport, but he's ⁶_____ at the bottom of the wardrobe. I'm nearly ready to go. I've ⁷_____ the things I want to take, but I ⁸_____ them in my bag yet.

1 a begin   b began   c begun
2 a got   b gets   c get
3 a she   b she's   c she hasn't
4 a is   b was   c has been
5 a can't   b couldn't   c hasn't
6 a just found it b found it yet c found it already
7 a choose   b chose   c chosen
8 a put   b didn't put c haven't put

4 Make questions for these answers. Use the present perfect.

1 *Has David done his homework?*

1 A: David / his homework?
   B: No, he hasn't done it yet.
2 A: you / just?
   B: Yes, I arrived a few minutes ago.
3 A: they / to the leisure centre recently?
   B: Yes, they went there yesterday.
4 A: How many times / you / a volcano?
   B: I've never seen one.
5 A: Nadia isn't here. She's gone out.
   B: Where / she?
   A: She's gone to the supermarket.

5 Complete the conversations with suggestions. Use your imagination.

1 A: I'm really tired.
   B: _____
2 A: This programme isn't very good, is it?
   B: No, it's boring.
   A: _____
3 A: Are you thirsty?
   B: Yes, I am.
   A: _____
4 A: I don't know how to get to Linda's place tomorrow.
   B: _____
5 A: What do you want to do on Saturday?
   B: I don't know. Have you got any suggestions?
   A: _____

6 How do you say these sentences in your language?

1 Sorry I haven't written recently.
2 She sends you her love.
3 What else has happened?
4 What will the weather be like tomorrow?
5 How's it going?
6 The horse has broken its leg.

Extra reading

Non-stop news

Would you like to visit a TV studio to see how a programme is made? What sort of programme would you choose?

There are hundreds of 24-hour news channels now. This is a typical day for one of them.

1 At the head office in London, the day begins with a meeting. The news team decides which stories to use, and how to treat them. News arrives all the time, night and day, so stories are often dropped and replaced by the latest headlines.

2 Reporters and camera operators work all over the UK, and around the world. When a reporter has recorded a story, he or she uses an 'outside broadcast' van to send it back to the studio. The dish on top of the van sends it via a satellite, 36 km above the earth.

3 In London, editors listen to the reports and watch the videos. When they have created the final news report, they give it a code and put it into a machine called a 'Betacart'. Then it is ready to use.

4 In the main newsroom, teams of journalists check the news as it comes in and write the scripts for the presenter.

5 The 'gallery' is where the director and his or her team put the final programme together. Sometimes, if an important story has just come in, there isn't time to prepare a script – so the team has to work very fast to choose facts, pictures and interviews.

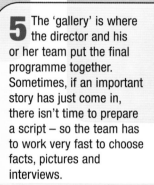

6 In the studio, the presenter reads the headlines. Presenters use an 'autocue' screen, which is on the camera in front of them. At the same time, the director in the gallery gives them instructions, so they often have to talk and listen at the same time. Presenters can never be sure what will happen, but they have to look cool and calm in every situation!

ABOUT TV

Fifty years ago, there were about five million TVs in the world. Today, there are about 1,000 million.

Task

Read the text, then find the name of the person who:

1 interviews people and sends stories to the studio.
2 films the news reports.
3 works at the studio and makes the final video.
4 writes the script for the presenter.
5 puts the final programme together.
6 reads the headlines on TV.

6 Attachments

1900

STEP 1

In Step 1 you study	so that you can
● present perfect with *for* and *since*	● talk about things in the present that started in the past
● time expressions	● give details about your background

1 Share your ideas

Does anyone that you know come from abroad or from a different part of the country?

> My grandparents weren't born here. They come from Algeria.

2 Presentation
They've been there for 100 years

a 🔲 Listen to the conversation and follow in your book. Who are the people and places in the photos?

Nadia's relatives moved to England from Poland many years ago. Luke's asking her about them.

LUKE: How long has your family been in England, Nadia?

NADIA: Oh, for ages! Since the 1940s. My great-grandparents came here during the war. So I've lived here all my life.

LUKE: Have you still got relatives in Poland?

NADIA: Yes, we have. We went to visit them about ten years ago. We haven't seen them for a long time now, but we keep in touch by email. I've got relatives in the USA too.

LUKE: Have you?

NADIA: Yes. Thousands of people from Eastern Europe emigrated to the USA. Some of my relatives moved there from Gdańsk in about 1900. They started a business in New York. They've been there for over 100 years now. We've never met them, but I'd love to visit them one day.

LUKE: And haven't you got an uncle in Canada?

NADIA: That's right – Mum's brother, Otto. She hasn't seen him since he left England, but they've written to each other every month for the last 12 years!

1943

b Read the conversation again. For each of these sentences, write **T** (true), **F** (false) or **?** (the text doesn't say).

1 Nadia's family has recently arrived in England.
2 Nadia was born in Liverpool.
3 All her relatives have left Poland.
4 She hasn't contacted her relatives in Poland for a long time.
5 Some of her relatives moved to New York.
6 Nadia has been to New York to see them.
7 Nadia's uncle lives in Ottawa.
8 Her mother started writing to him 12 years ago.

3 Key grammar
Present perfect with for *and* since

Read the examples and complete the explanation with *for* and *since*.

> They've lived in the USA **since** 1900.
> Otto has been in Canada **since** he left England.
> He's lived there **for** 12 years.
>
> *We can use the present perfect to describe a present situation that started in the past.*
> *We use _____ to show a period of time.*
> *We use _____ to say when the period of time started.*

G ► 5a–b

4 Practice

For each situation, write one sentence with present perfect + *for* and one with present perfect + *since*.

1 Karim has lived in Liverpool for twenty years. He's lived there since 19... .

1 Karim lives in Liverpool. He moved there twenty years ago.
2 Nadia's parents have got a boat. They bought it in 2004.
3 Andy bought his motorbike six years ago, when he was nineteen.
4 Beth doesn't play hockey now. She stopped five years ago, when she left school.
5 Luke doesn't eat meat. He stopped eating it when he was seven. He's eighteen now.

5 Key expressions *Time expressions*

for ages	for a fortnight
since Wednesday	since I arrived
six months ago	a long time ago
during 2005	during the war

a Replace the underlined words. Use *for, since, ago* or *during* + these words.

the night	ten minutes	a fortnight	an hour
five days	the winter	a long time	April

1 We've had a flat in London since April.

1 It's October now. We've had a flat in London <u>for six months</u>.
2 It's ten past eight. The film started <u>at eight o'clock</u>.
3 Luke and Nadia have known each other <u>since they were three</u>.
4 Danny left <u>at midday</u>. It's one o'clock now.
5 We don't often go to the beach <u>between November and March</u>.
6 Clare's cousin has been in Liverpool <u>for two weeks</u>.
7 I woke up several times <u>between midnight and five o'clock</u>.
8 Mr and Mrs Gray have been in Thailand <u>since Sunday</u>. It's Friday today.

b **Test a friend** Write another sentence for 5a. Leave a blank in place of *for, since, during* or *ago*. Can your friend complete the sentence?

Felix and I have known each other .... a long time.

6 Listening and speaking
There's no place like home

Rod Davenport is a surfing champion. He comes from St Ives in Cornwall.

a 🔲 Listen to the interview with Rod. Where is his favourite beach?

b 🔲 Copy the information, listen again and then complete the details.

ROD DAVENPORT	
[1] Two. months ago	won the European Longboard Championship
1985	born in [2] ....
[3]199.....	met his [4] ...., Tania
[5]20.....	became a professional surfer
Favourite place	[6] ....

🔲 Listen and check your answers.

c Ask and answer questions about Rod.

How long has he known Tania?

7 Speaking *About you*

Use what you know

Tell the class about yourself.

I was born in ... , ... years ago.
I've lived in ... for/since ...
I've known ... for/since ...
My favourite place is ...

In Step 2 you study
- words for personal possessions
- present perfect with superlative adjectives + *ever*
- *give* + direct and indirect object

so that you can
- describe important things and events
- talk about your possessions

1 Key vocabulary *Personal possessions*

⏱ Match the words with the pictures. You've got two minutes!

brush   comb   earrings   key ring   MP3 player
photo album   purse   wallet   watch

🔊 Listen and check.

2 Key pronunciation /ɜː/ /ɔː/

a 🔊 Listen and repeat the words. Find the odd one out in each group.

1 /ɜː/   purse   work   bird   bed
2 /ɔː/   walk   watch   bored   door

b 🔊 Now listen to some more words and repeat. Is the sound 1 or 2?

3 Presentation *My most precious possession*

a 🔊 Close your book and listen to Winston, Clare, Karim and Beth. What are their most precious possessions?

Winston
I've got three trumpets but this one's the best. It used to belong to a jazz player in Trinidad. I've had it since I was fourteen. It's definitely my most precious possession.

Clare
I've got hundreds of photos and I always put the best ones in an album. They're really important to me because they're souvenirs of all my happiest memories.

Karim
Leaving my home and family in Pakistan was the hardest thing I've ever done. Before I left, my father gave me this watch. It isn't the most valuable thing I own, but it's the most important to me.

Beth
My most precious possession is my engagement ring. Andy gave it to me on my twenty-first birthday. He's the nicest, funniest, most amazing person I've ever known.

b 🔊 Listen again and follow in your book. Why is each possession important to the person who owns it?

4 Key grammar *Present perfect with superlative adjectives + ever*

Read the example and complete the explanation.

> It was **the hardest** thing I've **ever** done.
> *We often use the present perfect +* .... *after the superlative.*
>
> *We also use* ever *in questions:*
> What's the hardest thing you've **ever** done?

 6

Remember!

Superlative adjectives
hard > hard**est**   nice > nic**est**
funny > funn**iest**   precious > **most** precious
amazing > **most** amazing
good > **best**   bad > **worst**

5 Practice

a Make questions using the superlative + *you've ever ...* .

1 What's the worst film you've ever seen?

1 What / bad film / see ?
2 Who / nice person / meet ?
3 Who / good actor / see ?
4 What / interesting book / read ?
5 What / funny TV programme / watch ?
6 What / amazing thing / do ?

b **What about you?** Work with a friend. Choose at least three questions from 5a. Ask and answer.

> What's the worst film you've ever seen?

> *The Adventures of Sharkboy.* It was awful!

If you have time, think of more questions using superlative adjectives.

> **Try this!**
> Find six more personal possessions.
> **CALCUBALAGTORCAMREINGRA DICTIOMONARYBILE**

6 Key grammar
give + direct and indirect object

How do you say these sentences in your language?

> Karim's father **gave Karim** a watch.
> Karim's father **gave him** a watch.
> Karim's father **gave it to him**.

 24a–c

7 Practice

a Make sentences with *Can you give it/them to me/him/her/them?*

1 Can you give them to her, please?

1 These are Maria's sunglasses.
2 These are Roberto's football boots.
3 This is Luke and Chris's CD.
4 This is Ana's rucksack.
5 That is my dictionary.

b Think of an interesting present for the person sitting next to you. Write it on a piece of paper and give it to him/her. Then take it in turns to say what you've got.

> Rosa has given me a Porsche!

8 Speaking *Your things*

Use what you know

Work in a group. Describe your most precious possession. How long have you had it? What's it like? Why is it important to you? Then decide which possession is:

– the most useful.
– the most unusual.
– the funniest.

> We think the most unusual thing is Eva's Moroccan key ring.

STEP 3

In Step 3 you
● read an interview
● study *still* and *any more*
so that you can
● write a personal account

1 Share your ideas *Changes*

What's the biggest change that has ever happened in your life? Did you enjoy making the change or was it difficult?

> When I was seven, we moved to a new flat. I wasn't very happy at first.

2 Reading

a Reading skills *Skimming*

🕐 Read the text quickly. You've got two minutes!

Now answer these questions. Don't look at the text.

1 The interview is with someone who …
  a has lived in several different countries.
  b lives in Canada.

2 Craig …
  a is a teenager at school.
  b works all over the world.

3 He's lived abroad for a … time.
  a short
  b long

4 He thinks that travelling is …
  a interesting.
  b boring.

5 He … to live in Canada all the time.
  a wants
  b doesn't want

On the move

Craig Forster is Canadian, but his father is an engineer who works all over the world. At the moment Craig and his family are living in Penang, in Malaysia. We asked him about his experiences.

How long have you been away from Canada?

We've only been in Penang for three months, but I've lived abroad for a long time. Since I was twelve I've lived in three different countries: Russia, Greece and now Malaysia.

That means you've been to lots of different schools?

Yes, that's right.

Has that been difficult?

Well, I've been at international schools which give lessons in English. But yes, it's difficult when you start at a new school in a foreign country. You don't know anyone and you feel a bit lost. The first time was the worst – that was in Russia. I was really confused and lonely for a while. And then, when I started to feel at home, Dad got a new job and we moved again!

So what's it like now in Penang?

I think I've adapted quite well and I've started to learn Malay. Of course I'm still a foreigner, but I don't mind that any more.

Have you enjoyed moving from place to place?

Yes and no. It's always interesting and it gives you confidence. But it's hard when you have to leave and say goodbye.

Do you ever go back to Canada?

Oh, yes. In fact I went back to my old school in Winnipeg for six months last year. In some ways that was the strangest experience I've ever had. Everything was the same, but I was different! I felt a lot older than other kids of my age.

Is Canada still 'home' to you?

I still love Winnipeg. But I don't really miss it any more, and it would be quite hard to live there all the time. I guess travelling is in my blood now!

b Comprehension check

🔲 Listen, and read the text again. For each of these sentences, write T (true), F (false) or ? (the text doesn't say).

1　Craig started living abroad three months ago.
2　He's had English-speaking teachers in foreign countries.
3　He was very unhappy when he first went to Russia.
4　Now he can speak Russian and Greek.
5　Craig thinks he's become more confident during the last five years.
6　Last year in Winnipeg, he was in a class with younger students.
7　He keeps in touch with his Canadian friends.
8　He'll probably continue to travel in the future.

3 Word work still, any more

Look at the examples.

I **still** love Winnipeg.
But I don't really miss it **any more**.

Match 1–5 with a–e. Then complete sentences a–e with *still* or *any more*.

1b My stereo is ten years old but it still works well.

1　My stereo is ten years old
2　Nadia's parents used to speak a bit of Polish
3　Has Winston left Mandela Court
4　Clare bought her first photo album ten years ago
5　Craig sometimes goes back to Winnipeg

a　or does he .... live there?
b　but it .... works well.
c　but he doesn't feel at home there ....
d　and she's .... got it.
e　but they can't remember much ....

Writing guide *A personal account*

● **Paragraph 1**
  Describe your early experiences.

  I left (place) *... years/months ago.*
  At first I ...
  I missed ...

● **Paragraph 2**
  Describe your life now.

  I've been in (place) *now for ...*
  I like / don't like ...
  I still miss ... / I don't miss ... any more.

4 Writing *A new life*

Use what you know

Look at the interview with Craig again. Imagine that you have recently left your home town to start a new life somewhere else. (Perhaps this is something that has really happened to you.) Write a personal account of your experiences and feelings.

When did you leave your original home?
How did you feel?
What's your life like now?

Extra exercises

1 Choose the right answer.

1 How long have you been here?
   a Nearly two hours ago.
   b Since midday.
   c At five o'clock.

2 When did they emigrate to Australia?
   a During the war.
   b For 15 years.
   c Since 1995.

3 Has Alan contacted you recently?
   a No, he didn't.
   b No, I haven't.
   c No, not for a long time.

4 What was your holiday like?
   a Yes, I did. I had a great time.
   b It was the best one I've ever had.
   c We're going to go to Istanbul.

5 Do they live in Peru?
   a Yes, they've been there for two years now.
   b Yes, they lived there for five years.
   c Yes, they are.

2 Put the letters in the right order and make words for personal possessions. Then use the words to complete the sentences.

THAWC   WELTLA   SNAGRERI   BOCM   HOTOP BLUMA   YEK GRIN

1 My hair's a mess, but I can't find my ....
2 Lorina often wears silver ....
3 What time is it? I haven't got a ....
4 I've got a little light on my .... so I can see to open the door.
5 I'm going to put all my holiday photos in a ....
6 I think I've lost my .... ! It's got £25 in it.

3 Read the text and choose the right word(s) for each space.

I've known Sam [1]............ we were at primary school, and [2]............ friends for a long time. He's one of the nicest people I've ever [3]............ . He and his family [4]............ to Manchester six months ago, and now we [5]............ each other very often. But we've kept in touch by email, and [6]............ a fortnight with him in Manchester during the holidays. It was great to see him again.

1 a since   b when   c while
2 a we're   b we aren't   c we've been
3 a met   b knew   c liked
4 a move   b moved   c have moved
5 a don't see   b didn't see c haven't seen
6 a I spend   b I spent   c I've spent

4 Make sentences with the superlative and *ever*.

1 *It's the biggest surfboard I've ever seen.*

1 That surfboard is enormous. (*big/see*)
2 These trainers are fantastic. (*comfortable/buy*)
3 Sylvia's a great friend. (*good/have*)
4 It's a really stupid song. (*silly/hear*)
5 This pizza is horrible. (*bad/eat*)
6 That girl really annoys me. (*annoying/know*)

5 Put the words in the right order and make sentences.

1 *Give Ana the purse.*

1 Ana / the purse / give
2 we / Clare / some earrings / gave
3 it / give / to me
4 me / give / the tickets
5 it / gave / to her / they
6 to us / didn't / them / give / she
7 father / it / to him / Karim's / gave
8 Luke / gave / I / wallet / your

6 How do you say these sentences in your language?

1 I've lived in England all my life.
2 They've been here for ages.
3 They left during the winter.
4 We keep in touch by email.
5 Have you still got relatives in Nairobi?
6 They often write to each other.

Extra reading

New Zealand

Life and culture

How far is your country from New Zealand?
What do you know about it?

Facts

Capital city Wellington
Population 4.2 million
Main languages English, Maori
Currency New Zealand dollar
Main exports wool, cheese, butter, meat

North Island · Auckland
Cook Strait
Wellington
South Island · Christchurch · Mount Cook
Pacific Ocean

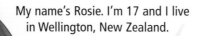

My name's Rosie. I'm 17 and I live in Wellington, New Zealand.

Wellington is by the sea so we spend a lot of time at the beach. My friends are crazy about surfing but I'm scared of big waves, so I just watch! Outdoor activities are very popular in New Zealand, and bungee-jumping began here.

I guess my favourite thing about Wellington is that it's so multicultural. I have friends whose families come from Tonga and Fiji in the South Pacific, and from India, Japan and Germany.

I love drinking coffee and chatting to my friends. There are hundreds of cafés in Wellington. The best one I've been to is called 'The Chocolate Fish'. When they were filming *The Lord of the Rings*, the cast and crew used to relax there at the weekend, so we collected a lot of autographs.

The national symbol of New Zealand is the kiwi – a bird which has very small wings and can't fly. There are also some strange lizards called *tuataras*. They've been here for two hundred million years!

The Maoris were the first inhabitants of New Zealand. They came from Polynesia and they've been here for about a thousand years. The Europeans arrived much later – about 200 years ago – and at first there were fierce battles between the Maoris and the Europeans. I'm learning Maori at school (but a lot of people also learn Japanese as a second language), and my favourite subject is Pacific art.

New Zealand is great but it's quite isolated so, when I finish school, I want to spend a year travelling round Europe.

ABOUT NEW ZEALANDERS

People who live in New Zealand are often called 'Kiwis' – after the bird that lives there.

Task

Read the facts and the text, then read these sentences. Are the sentences true or false? Correct the false sentences.

1 The population of New Zealand is very big.
2 Rosie often goes surfing.
3 New Zealanders spend a lot of their free time outdoors.
4 Chocolate fish is a popular dessert in New Zealand.
5 The stars of *The Lord of the Rings* used to go to a café in Wellington.
6 The kiwi is an unusual bird.
7 The first settlers were from Europe.
8 Japanese is a popular second language in schools.

Grammar check

1 Present perfect and past simple
Work it out for yourself

Look at the pictures and complete the explanations. Use *past simple* and *present perfect*.

Present perfect

The President has died.

Past simple

When did he die? Where did he die?

Past simple

He died last night at the presidential palace.

1 We use the _____ when we're interested in the present result of a past event.
2 We use the _____ when we ask for or give details about a past event.
3 We don't use a past time expression (*last night*, *yesterday*, etc.) with the _____ .

Check that you can

• understand the difference between the present perfect and the past simple.

Complete the dialogues. Use the present perfect or the past simple.

1 A: Where's Fiona?
   B: She *'s gone* (go) to Tokyo. She _____ (leave) yesterday.

2 A: _____ (you/see) my wallet? I can't find it.
   B: Yes, I _____ (see) it this morning. It _____ (be) on the table in the hall.

3 A: A fire _____ (destroy) the leisure centre.
   B: That's terrible. Are you sure?
   A: Yes, I _____ (hear) it on the ten o'clock news.

4 A: Come and eat your breakfast!
   B: I can't. I _____ (not finish) my homework. I _____ (not have) time to do it last night.

2 Present perfect + *just, yet* and *already*
Work it out for yourself

A Look at the Arrivals board and complete the sentences with the correct flight number.

BRISTOL AIRPORT
18:23
ARRIVALS

FLIGHT	FROM		
BA 654	LONDON	ARRIVED	17:35
IB 973	MADRID	EXPECTED	18:40
AF 312	PARIS	ARRIVED	18:21

1 Flight _____ has just arrived.
2 Flight _____ has already arrived.
3 Flight _____ hasn't arrived yet.

B Complete the explanations. Use *already, just* and *yet*.

1 We use _____ for things that were completed before now.
2 We use _____ in negative sentences and questions when we expect something to happen.
3 We use _____ for something that happened a short time ago.

Check that you can

• use *just, yet* and *already*.

Make sentences using the present perfect + *just, yet, already*.

1 *I've just painted it.*

1 Don't touch that door! I (just / paint / it).
2 A: You must tidy your room.
   B: I (already / tidy / it).
3 The TV's better now. We (just / buy) a new satellite dish.
4 Don't throw that magazine away. I (not read / it / yet).
5 (you finish / your breakfast / yet)?
6 They don't want to watch the film. They (already / see / it).

3 Present perfect + *for* and *since*

Work it out for yourself

A Read the dialogue, then choose the right words in sentences 1–3.

WOMAN: *How long* have you been there?

MAN: *I've been* here for ages, *since* about ten o'clock this morning.

1 The man *is / has been* there since ten o'clock.
2 He *doesn't move / hasn't moved* for six hours.
3 He has been there *for / since* he fell.

B Complete the explanations.

1 We use the .... + *for* and *since* to talk about situations that started in the past and are continuing now.
2 We use .... to give a period of time, and .... to say when a period of time started.

Check that you can

- say how long something has continued.

Complete the sentences using *for* or *since*.

1 I'm really hungry. I haven't eaten ...*since*... midday.
2 Is the dog OK? It hasn't moved .... the last two hours.
3 My brother has lived in Australia .... he emigrated in 2004.
4 I haven't been to the cinema .... ages.
5 The weather has been hot .... the beginning of June.
6 I've known my best friend .... ten years.

4 Superlatives + present perfect with *ever*

Work it out for yourself

Read the sentences, then answer the question.

*She's **the nicest** person I've **ever known**.*
*It's **the most difficult** thing Kate **has ever done**.*
What tense do we use with the superlative + *ever*?

Check that you can

- use the superlative + present perfect with *ever*.

Make questions for these answers.

1 What's the strangest thing you've ever eaten?

1 A: strange / eat? B: Snake meat.
2 A: good / buy? B: My mobile phone.
3 A: exciting / do? B: I did a bungee-jump last year.
4 A: beautiful / see? B: A sunset in the mountains.

5 *give* + direct and indirect object

Work it out for yourself

Lucy has bought some Christmas presents.

*'I'll give **my sister the earrings**. And Adam? I'll give **him the DVD**. Shall I give **the key ring to Dad**? Yes, I'll give **it to him**. And Olivia? I'll give **her the chocolates**.'*

Look at Lucy's sentences, then complete the explanations with *direct* or *indirect*.

1 We often put the indirect object **before** the .... object. (*I'll give **Adam/him the DVD**.*)
2 But we can put the .... object (with *to*) **after** the .... object. (*I'll give **it/the DVD to Adam/to him**.*)

Check that you can

- use *give* + a direct and an indirect object.

Put the words in the right order and make sentences.

1 I gave Sarah a birthday present.

1 Sarah / I / birthday / gave / present / a
2 me / present / a / gave / Carmen
3 gave / Miguel / ticket / I / my
4 A: Is this your MP3 player?
   B: No. me / to / Leo / it / gave
5 A: What shall I do with these old CDs?
   B: them / friends / to / give / your

Vocabulary and expressions

Topics in the news
crime
famous people
health
politics
sport
the environment
the weather
war and peace

Offers and suggestions
I could read …
Shall I ask …?
Why don't you give me …?
You could give me …

Yellowstone Park
alive
ash
earthquake
(to) erupt
eruption
fascinated
geyser
giant
hot spring
(to) increase
movement
over (= on top of)

Time expressions
a long time ago
during 2005
during the war
for a fortnight
for ages
since I arrived
since Wednesday
six months ago

Personal possessions
brush
comb
earrings
key ring
MP3 player
photo album
purse
wallet
watch

Living abroad
(to) adapt
(to) be away from
confused
(to) feel at home
foreigner
in some ways
It's in my blood.
lonely
(to) move (house)

Study skills 3 Homophones

Homophones are words which have the same sound but different spelling and meaning, for example:

I love boats and my ambition is to *sail* across the Atlantic.
Our neighbours are moving. The house next door is for *sale*.

⏱ **Find a homophone for at least five of the following words. You've got two minutes!**

1	right	5	weigh	9	hour
2	sea	6	threw	10	nose
3	their	7	know	11	wear
4	wood	8	meat	12	knew

Write sentences to show the meaning of three of the pairs of homophones that you've found.

How's it going?

● **Your rating**

Look again at pages 66 and 67. For each section decide on your rating: Good ✓✓✓   Not bad ✓✓   I can't remember much ✓

● **Vocabulary**

Choose one topic from the Vocabulary list then close your book. How many words can you remember?

● **Test a friend**

Look again at Units 5 and 6. Think of at least two questions, then ask a friend.

> Why did Danny's mother buy him a suit?

> What's Clare's most important possession?

● **Correcting mistakes**

Can you correct these mistakes? In some sentences, there is more than one mistake.

1 ~~I've bought some new trainers yesterday. Are you like them?~~
2 ~~I'm bored. We go out?~~
3 ~~Mel is in London now. She works there during six months.~~
4 ~~What's the most good film you ever seen?~~
5 ~~I've never met a so rude person.~~

● **Your Workbook**

Complete the Learning Diaries for Units 5 and 6.

Coursework 3 — Our school magazine

Read the reviews in this month's edition of *Pulse*. Then choose a book, a film or a TV programme that you've enjoyed and write a review.

Reviews ★ ★ ★ ★ ★ ★ ★

If you want to know about the best books, films and TV programmes, here are the latest reviews from some of our readers.

Books

The Curious Incident of the Dog in the Night-Time by Mark Haddon is the best book I've read for a long time. I couldn't put it down! It's about a 15-year-old boy called Christopher Boone, who has Asperger's Syndrome. He's brilliant at maths but he finds ordinary life very difficult. Christopher discovers his neighbour's dog dead in the garden next door, and his neighbour thinks that he killed it. Christopher decides to find the real killer, and he makes some interesting discoveries on the way. This isn't just a good story; it helps you to understand the problems of people with learning difficulties. Buy it, borrow it or get it from the library – but make sure you read it!

Ellie East   Year 9

Films

I've seen *The Incredibles* three times now and I love it! It's fast, exciting and very funny. At the beginning of the film, the Parrs – Bob, Helen, Violet, Dash and Jack-Jack – look like an ordinary American family. Bob has a boring job in an office, but he used to be a superhero called Mr Incredible and his family all have special powers too. One day Bob gets the chance to be a superhero again and defeat an evil robot …
Holly Hunter and Craig T. Nelson play the parts of the parents and Samuel L. Jackson is their friend Frozone. They're all excellent.

Alex Turner   Year 11

TV

I've just watched the first part of *Life in the Undergrowth*, a new series about insects by David Attenborough. Yes, insects! Boring? No way! They're incredible creatures and it's one of the most interesting programmes I've ever seen. The camera operators use the latest high-tech equipment and the results are amazing. Attenborough travels to the four corners of the planet to bring us his fantastic pictures and fascinating reports. Don't miss it! It's on BBC1 on Wednesdays at nine o'clock.

Anthony Wall   Year 12

Module 4

Talking points

In Module 4 Steps 1 and 2 you study

Grammar
- First conditional with *if* and *unless*
- The future with *will* and *going to*
- *might* and *may*
- *when* in future sentences
- *should*
- Second conditional

Vocabulary
- Special occasions
- Verbs and nouns that go together

Expressions
- *I hope so/not. I guess so/not.*
- Responding to opinions

so that you can
- Describe special occasions
- Talk about results
- Talk about superstitions
- Talk about events in the future and future plans
- React to what other people say
- Talk about things that aren't certain
- Say when things will happen in the future
- Talk about what's right and wrong
- Talk about hypothetical situations

Life and culture
The number 13
The code talkers

Coursework 4

Part 4 Letters to the editor
You write a letter for a magazine letters page.

editor

why not write?
ulse Magazine,
nside Road,

/ violence

ar Editors,
ults often say there's too
ch violence on TV and in
mputer games, for example
eetfighter. But, in my
inion, it's not true that
ung people think violence is
rmal because we see it on
r screens. I hate violence.
The news on TV is often as
lent as computer games but

Mrs Massey

We want to say a big THANK
YOU to Mrs Massey, who is
leaving at the end of the term.
She has been our history
teacher for three years and we
all think she's brilliant.
    Mrs Massey, you're one in a
million! Thanks for everything.
We wish you all the very best.

Year 11 History Group

In Step 3 you ...

read
- Invitations and replies
- An article about a 'con man'

study
- Verbs with *look*
- *because, so*
- Scanning a text for information
- Predicting the topic of a text

so that you can
- Write an invitation and a reply
- Write an imaginary 'sales talk'

What's it about?

What can you say about the pictures?

Now match the pictures with sentences 1–5.

1 If you found a friend's diary, what would you do?
2 You'll have to wear something interesting.
3 Beth's going to get married tomorrow.
4 If you swim in the sea on Good Friday, you'll turn into a fish.
5 She might spend the day outside someone's house.

7 Celebrations

In Step 1 you study
- words for special occasions
- first conditional with *if* and *unless*

so that you can
- describe special occasions
- talk about results
- talk about superstitions

Try this!
How many words can you make with these letters?
CELEBRATION
brain, …

1 Key vocabulary *Special occasions*

a Look at these expressions. How do you say them in your language?

1 Happy birthday
2 Happy New Year
3 Congratulations!
4 Happy anniversary
5 Good luck!

b Match the words with the pictures.

cake   candles   costumes   decorations
fireworks   guests   presents   procession

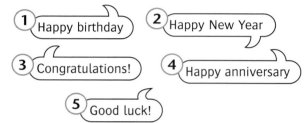

Listen and check.

c Think of at least one special occasion in your country for each word in 1b.

cake: wedding, birthday

2 Key pronunciation *Final /s/ and /z/*

a Listen and repeat the words.

1 /s/ cakes guests trips presents
2 /z/ costumes meals parties weddings

b Now listen to some more words and repeat. Is the final sound /s/ or /z/?

3 Presentation
If you do that, you'll turn into a fish.

a What can you say about the pictures?

b Read the text. Which words or phrases refer to special occasions?

c Match 1–7 with a–g and make seven superstitions.

1b If you see a spider in your home, you'll soon have guests.

Listen and check your answers.

4 Key grammar
First conditional with if *and* unless

Complete the examples and read the explanations.

> **If** you **swim** on Good Friday, you _____ **turn into** a fish.
>
> *We use* If + present simple, and *will/won't + verb to describe the result of a possible future action.*
>
> **Unless** you _____ something red on your wedding day, you won't be happy.
> **Unless** you wear = **If** you **don't** wear
>
> *We can change the order of the two parts of the sentence:*
> You'll turn into a fish if you swim on Good Friday.
> You won't be happy unless you wear something red on your wedding day.

G 13a–b

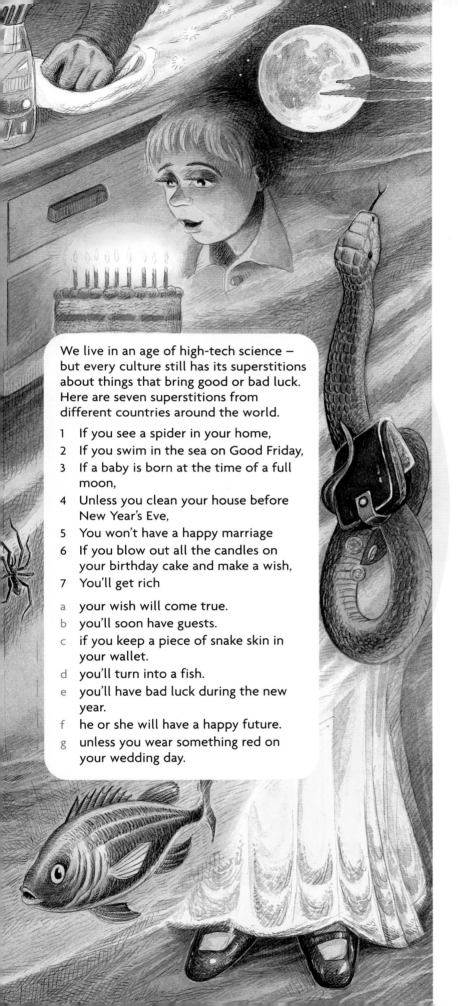

We live in an age of high-tech science – but every culture still has its superstitions about things that bring good or bad luck. Here are seven superstitions from different countries around the world.

1 If you see a spider in your home,
2 If you swim in the sea on Good Friday,
3 If a baby is born at the time of a full moon,
4 Unless you clean your house before New Year's Eve,
5 You won't have a happy marriage
6 If you blow out all the candles on your birthday cake and make a wish,
7 You'll get rich

a your wish will come true.
b you'll soon have guests.
c if you keep a piece of snake skin in your wallet.
d you'll turn into a fish.
e you'll have bad luck during the new year.
f he or she will have a happy future.
g unless you wear something red on your wedding day.

5 Practice

a Complete the sentences with *if* or *unless*.

1 .... it's a nice day tomorrow, we'll have lunch outside.
2 What will we do .... it rains?
3 The bus is late. We'll miss the beginning of the film .... it comes soon.
4 .... you ring me from the station, I'll come and meet you.
5 That plant will die .... you give it some water.

b Complete the sentences. Use the right form of the verbs.

1 If you .... (*visit*) our town during the carnival, you .... (*have*) a great time.
2 If my brother .... (*pass*) his exams, we .... (*organise*) a big celebration.
3 I .... (*not go*) to the party unless you .... (*come*) with me.
4 If it .... (*not be*) too hot on Saturday, we .... (*have*) a barbecue on the beach.
5 We .... (*not be able to*) dance unless someone .... (*bring*) a CD player.
6 David's meal .... (*be*) cold if he .... (*not come*) soon.
7 I .... (*not listen*) to you unless you .... (*stop*) shouting.

6 Writing and speaking
Superstitions

Use what you know

Write two or three superstitions. Then read out the first part of each sentence.

If you break a mirror, ...

Can other people in the class complete it?

Do you believe in any of these superstitions?

In Step 2 you study
- the future with *will* and *going to*
- *I hope so/not. I guess so/not.*

so that you can
- talk about events in the future and future plans
- react to what other people say

1 Share your ideas

Have you ever been to a wedding? Did you enjoy it? Can you describe what happens at a typical wedding in your country?

People often get married in the town hall.

2 Presentation *They're going to get married*

a 📼 Close your book and listen to the conversation. Which of these things is Mrs Gray worrying about?

presents guests the wedding cake
decorations the video camera

It's the day before Beth and Andy's wedding. They're getting married at eleven o'clock tomorrow and they're having the reception at a local hotel.

BETH: Mum, Andy's going to invite two more people – two of his old school friends. So there'll probably be two more at the reception.

MRS GRAY: Beth! There won't be enough room for them.

BETH: Don't worry, Mum. It won't be a problem.

MRS GRAY: Well, I hope not. I've just had a call from the baker's. They won't be able to finish the cake this afternoon. We'll have to pick it up tomorrow morning.

BETH: Who's going to pick it up?

DANNY: Shall I get it? Andy could take me on his motorbike.

BETH: My wedding cake on the back of Andy's motorbike? No way!

MR GRAY: I'll get it, Beth. I'll go after breakfast. OK?

BETH: Yes, I guess so. Thanks, Dad.

MRS GRAY: Barry, have you checked the batteries in the video camera?

MR GRAY: No, but I haven't forgotten. I'm going to look at it after dinner.

DANNY: I'll do it now if you like. Mum, relax! Everything will be fine!

MRS GRAY: Oh, I hope so!

b 📼 Listen again and follow in your book. Find answers to these questions.

1 What has Andy decided to do?
2 Why does Mrs Gray think it'll be a problem?
3 Is Beth worried about it?
4 When will the cake be ready?
5 Who's going to pick it up?
6 When's he going to get it?
7 What does Danny offer to do now?

3 Key grammar
The future with will *and* going to

Look at the examples and complete the explanations with *will, won't* or *going to*.

> The cake **won't be** ready this afternoon. Everything **will be** fine.
>
> *We use* _____ *('ll) or* _____ *+ verb for future facts and predictions.*
>
> **I'll get** the cake tomorrow morning.
>
> *We use* _____ *('ll) + verb when we decide to do something at the time of speaking. We often use* I'll *when we offer to do something.*
>
> Andy**'s going to invite** two more people.
>
> *We use* _____ *+ verb to talk about our intentions when we've already decided what to do.*

 G ▶ 11a-b

4 Practice

a Choose the right words.

1 I've bought this poster for my room. (*I'll / I'm going to*) put it over my desk.

2 Clare's gone to the library. (*She'll / She's going to*) do her history essay.

3 Winston isn't here now, but I think (*he'll / he's going to*) be back soon.

4 Why don't we stop at the café? (*I'll / I'm going to*) buy you a cup of coffee.

5 Our neighbours have sold their house. (*They'll / They're going to*) move to Italy.

6 I'm making a salad. It (*won't / isn't going to*) take long.

b Work with a friend. Read out the dialogue between two of Beth and Andy's friends. Then choose different clothes and practise the dialogue again.

A: What are you going to wear to the wedding?

B: I'm going to wear my new suit. What about you?

A: I haven't decided yet. I'll probably wear my new skirt and my black jacket.

If you have time, make two more dialogues. Use these words.

What / give Beth and Andy?
How / get to the church?

5 Key expressions   I hope/guess so.

Complete the dialogues with these expressions.

I hope so.
I hope not.
I guess so.
I guess not.

1 A: Is Kevin going to wear his monkey costume tomorrow?

   B: Oh, _____ . It looks terrible!

2 A: Are they going to have any food at the party?

   B: _____ . I'm starving!

3 A: If you want to catch the last train, you'll have to leave soon.

   B: Yes, _____ .

4 A: We can send Martina an invitation, but she probably won't come.

   B: _____ . She doesn't really like parties.

6 Listening   Song

a 🔊 Listen to the song. What's going to happen?

b 🔊 Listen again. Match 1–6 with a–f and make lines from the song.

1	Birds	a	love you.
2	We're	b	will shine.
3	We're going to	c	going to the chapel.
4	I really	d	will sing.
5	Bells	e	get married.
6	The sun	f	will ring.

7 Writing and speaking
Describing a celebration

Use what you know

Write sentences about a celebration that's happening soon: a birthday, a wedding, a special family celebration or a festival in your town/ country.

What are your plans?
We're going to have some fireworks.

What will it be like?
I think it'll be fun.

Discuss your plans with a friend.

In Step 3 you
- read three invitations and replies
- study verbs with *look*

so that you can
- write an invitation and a reply

1 Share your ideas
Let's celebrate!

Think about special occasions in your country. Which ones are most important? What's your favourite day of the year?

> My favourite day is New Year's Eve. We sometimes have a fancy dress party.

2 Reading

a Read the texts quickly and match invitations 1–3 with replies a–c.

Listen and check your answers.

Barry and Lynette Gray
request the pleasure of your company
at the wedding of their daughter

Elizabeth
to
Andrew Perry

on Saturday 12th March
at 11.00 am

at St John's Church
2 Grange Road
Liverpool

and afterwards at the reception
at the Grand Hotel

RSVP
Mr and Mrs B Gray
3 Mandela Court
68 Hayle Road
Liverpool L10 1JB   Tel: 0151 111 6489

Dear …

This is just a short note to say that I'm having a party for my 18th birthday on Saturday 4th September. I hope you can come. It's going to be a fancy dress party, so you'll have to wear something interesting! There'll be a band and we'll be able to dance all night.

I know it won't be easy for you to get here from Scotland, but I'd love to see you. You could stay with us for the weekend.

Let me know if you can come.

Love,
Hannah

Hi …

Have you made any plans for Saturday yet? If not, would you like to come over to my place in the evening? Sam will be back from New Zealand and we're inviting a few people to welcome him home. Come for dinner, at about 7.30. If the weather's nice, we'll have a barbecue outdoors.

See you on Saturday, I hope.

Eddie

b **Reading skills** *Scanning*

Look at the three invitations and find answers to these questions. Don't read every word. You've got two minutes!

1 Where are Beth and Andy getting married?
2 Where will the wedding reception be?
3 What's the date of Hannah's party?
4 How old will she be?
5 What time are the guests arriving at Eddie's place?

c **Comprehension check**

Read the texts again and answer the questions.

1 Who is replying 'yes' to an invitation? Who is replying 'no'?
2 Which guest will wear a special costume?
3 What address will Alice use when she sends her reply?
4 Why will Adam be at home on Saturday evening?
5 How is Fiona going to travel to London?
6 Is Sam at home at the moment?

a

Hello there!

Thanks a lot for inviting me on Saturday, but I'm afraid I won't be able to come. My parents are going out and I've promised to stay at home and look after my sisters. Please say hi to Sam for me. I'll ring him at the weekend and hope to see him next week.

Adam

b

Dear ...

Thank you very much for your wedding invitation. I'd love to come. I know it will be a wonderful occasion and I'm really looking forward to it.

With best wishes from
Alice

c

Dear ...

Thanks very much for your invitation. The party sounds fantastic and I'd love to come. I'm going to get a train on Saturday morning, so I'll probably arrive at about three o'clock. Thanks also for inviting me to stay at your place – great! I'm looking forward to seeing you all.

Love
Fiona

3 Word work *Verbs with look*

a Complete the sentences with the verbs in the box.

| look up   look for   look at |
| look after   look forward to |
| look round |

1 Luke isn't well, so his dad's going to stay at home to .... him.
2 .... Jill's costume! It's fabulous.
3 Let's go into town and .... the shops.
4 If you don't understand a word, you can .... it .... in the dictionary.
5 We always .... the summer holidays.
6 I can't find my wallet. Could you help me to .... it?

b **Test a friend** Write a sentence for at least one of the verbs in 3a, but leave a blank. Can your friend complete the sentence?

I'm going to look ..... a birthday present for Mike.

Writing guide *Invitations and replies*

● Inviting
Would you like to come ...?
I hope you can come.
I'd love to see you.
Let me know if you can come.
RSVP (= Please reply)

● Replying
Thank you (very much) for the invitation.
Thanks (a lot) for inviting me.

● Accepting
I'd love to come.
I'm looking forward to it / to seeing you.

● Saying you can't come
I'd love to come, but ... / I'm really sorry, but ...
I'm afraid I won't be able to come.

4 Writing *An invitation and a reply*

Use what you know

Think about an invitation that a friend would like to receive, for example:

– An actor is inviting him/her to go to the Oscars award night in Hollywood.
– A football star is inviting him/her to watch the football World Cup final.

Write the invitation and give it to your friend. Then reply to the invitation that you receive.

Extra exercises

1 Read the text. Put the letters in order and make words describing special occasions.

When my sister Kate had her 18th birthday, we held a big fancy dress party. We invited about 50 ¹*stuges* and everyone wore funny ²*mescouts*. They all brought ³*drasc* and ⁴*sterpsen* for Kate. The house looked fantastic – there were ⁵*icrodanesto* everywhere. We danced until midnight and then Mum brought in a fabulous ⁶*ecka* with 18 ⁷*declans* on it. After that we had ⁸*sikorfrew* outside in the garden. It was a great celebration.

2 Complete the conversations.

1   A: We've been married for exactly five years.
    B: Happy .... !
    a birthday   b anniversary   c New Year

2   A: I'm playing in the hockey final this afternoon.
    B: ....
    a Good luck!   b Congratulations!   c I'm really sorry.

3   A: You've got a bad cold. You'll have to stay at home tonight, I'm afraid.
    B: I .... so.
    a agree   b hope   c guess

4   A: Will the tickets cost a lot?
    B: I .... I've only got £10.
    a hope so   b hope not   c guess not

5   A: Will you be able to play on Saturday?
    B: Yes, I .... so.
    a will   b can   c hope

6   A: Your parents won't be very pleased.
    B: No, I .... not.
    a guess   b won't   c guess so

3 Match 1–8 with a–h and make eight sentences.

1   People won't want to dance
2   If we can't mend this pan,
3   Unless it rains,
4   If you don't want that food,
5   How will we get home
6   What will you do
7   We won't have to go to the bank
8   I'll be annoyed

a   we'll have dinner on the balcony.
b   unless we run out of money.
c   we'll have to get a new one.
d   if I can't get a ticket for the concert.
e   if James doesn't get your message?
f   unless we have some good music.
g   I'll give it to the dog.
h   if we miss the last bus?

4 Complete the sentences. Choose *if* or *unless* and write the verb in the correct form.

1   *We won't go to Scott's wedding unless he invites us.*

1   We .... to Scott's wedding (*if / unless*) he invites us. (*not go*)

2   (*If / Unless*) you speak to me like that again, you .... go out this evening. (*not be able to*)

3   (*If / Unless*) Lesley .... to the café, she'll meet us outside the theatre. (*not come*)

4   You .... in trouble (*if / unless*) you turn off that awful music! (*be*)

5   Your wish won't come true (*if / unless*) you .... all the candles! (*not blow out*)

6   (*If / Unless*) Angelo .... more careful, he'll have an accident. (*be*)

5 Complete the sentences. Use the verbs with *will* or *going to*.

1   I .... some black boots. I've seen some nice ones in Clark's shoe shop. (*buy*)

2   Tony wants to learn Portuguese because he .... a year in Lisbon. (*spend*)

3   A: Have we got any orange juice?
    B: Probably. I .... a look. (*have*)

4   You shouldn't worry about the test. I promise it .... difficult. (*not be*)

5   We .... cook tonight because I've bought some fish and chips. (*not have to*)

6   A: I've lost one of my earrings.
    B: Oh, that's annoying. I .... you look for it. (*help*)

7   Don't try to solve that puzzle! You .... (*not succeed*)

8   Joanne has decided to move but she .... Liverpool. (*not leave*)

6 How do you say these sentences in your language?

1   Congratulations!
2   We'll have to pick it up tomorrow.
3   There won't be enough room for a piano.
4   No way!
5   Relax! Everything will be fine.
6   I'm looking forward to seeing you.

Extra reading

The number 13

Do people in your country believe that the number 13 is unlucky? What do you think?

- Many people believe that the number 13, and particularly the date Friday 13th, are unlucky. Fear of the number 13 is called *triskaidekaphobia*.

- In hotels, floor and room numbers often go from 12 to 14, and airlines sometimes do the same with seat numbers. A survey found that 41% of people in Britain worry if the date is Friday 13th. In hospitals, many people refuse to have an operation on that date.

- Every Friday 13th, the members of the Philadelphia Friday 13th Club in the USA have lunch together.

Afterwards, they break mirrors, walk under ladders, open umbrellas indoors and do lots of other 'unlucky' things.

- Robert Renphrey has had four accidents on Friday 13th. He has broken bones, fallen into a river, been injured by a motorbike and walked through a glass door. Now he stays in bed if the date is Friday 13th.

- Superstitious sailors often used to refuse to go to sea on Friday 13th. In 1791, the British government decided to prove that they were wrong. They started building a ship on Friday 13th. They called it *Friday* and its first journey began on a Friday. No one ever saw the ship or its crew again.

- The American President Franklin Roosevelt was very superstitious. He never travelled on the 13th of the month, unless he really had no choice.

- Some people believe that, if you have a party with 13 people, something bad will happen. Many years ago, at the Savoy Hotel in London, there were 13 guests at a dinner table. The host of the party later died. Since that time, when there is a group of 13 people having dinner at the hotel, the waiters make an extra place at the table for Kaspar, a black wooden cat.

ABOUT NUMBERS

The most popular lucky number is 7.

Task

Read the text, then answer the questions.

1 What percentage of British people believe that Friday 13th is unlucky?
2 Who tries to prove that they aren't afraid of Friday 13th?
3 Why does Robert Renphrey stay in bed on Friday 13th?
4 What happened to the ship *Friday*?
5 Why didn't Roosevelt like travelling on the 13th?
6 If you take 12 friends to dinner at the Savoy, what will the waiters do?
7 Who or what is Kaspar?

Secrets and lies

In Step 1 you study
- *might* and *may*
- *when* in future sentences

so that you can
- talk about things that aren't certain
- say when things will happen in the future

1 Share your ideas

Look at the woman in the photos. What do you think her job is? Give reasons for your answer.

> In the first photo, she's putting on make-up. Perhaps she's a/an .....

2 Presentation

What might tomorrow bring?

a  Listen to the interview with Mary Martin and follow in your book. Would you like to have Mary's job? Give reasons for your answer.

Mary Martin works as a private investigator in New York.

How long have you been a private investigator?
For eight years now. Before that, I used to work in the police department.

Tell us a bit about your daily routine.
There isn't a routine. You never know what might happen. Tomorrow, for example, I might get a phone call from a client and then I might spend the rest of the day outside someone's house. I may not finish until midnight. Sometimes I use a disguise, or change the way I speak. And I travel a lot. I may go abroad next week. I'm not sure yet. I'm, er, working for someone well known at the moment.

But you aren't going to give us any details?
No. I'm afraid I can't. But I might write a book when I retire. So, when you read my autobiography, you'll know all my secrets!

b Read the interview again. Match questions 1–5 with answers a–e. Then ask and answer.

1 Is Mary sure about what will happen tomorrow?
2 Where might she spend the day tomorrow?
3 Will she finish work at five?
4 Will she definitely go abroad next week?
5 When will we know all Mary's secrets?

a No. She might stay in New York.
b No, she isn't. She doesn't know what will happen.
c When she writes her book.
d She might. But it may be much later than that.
e Outside someone's house, perhaps.

3 Key grammar might *and* may

Read the examples and complete the explanation.

> I **might/may** go abroad next week. I'm not sure yet.
>
> *We use* _____ *or* _____ *to describe something in the future that isn't certain.*
>
> May *and* might *have the same meaning here, but in questions we usually use* might, *not* may.
> What **might** she do tomorrow?
>
> *We form the negative like this:*
> She **might not/may not** go abroad.

G ► 15

4 Practice

Think of someone you know, or someone famous, and imagine you're asking a private investigator to follow him/her. What might he/she do in the next few days?

He might go to a club called Mojo's on Friday. I'm not sure.

He may spend the weekend with his friend Ryan.

Try this!
Imagine you want to use a disguise. Make a list of things that you can use.

wig, ...

5 Key pronunciation /aɪ/ /eɪ/

a 🔘 Listen and repeat the words. Find the odd one out in each group.

1 /aɪ/ might eye white paid high
2 /eɪ/ may rain said eight gate

b Find three words for Group 1 and three words for Group 2. There are two odd ones out.

night day head wait size friend came why

🔘 Listen, check and repeat.

6 Key grammar when *in future sentences*

Read the example. Is it about the present or the future? Complete the explanation.

> **When** you **read** my autobiography, you'**ll know** all my secrets.
>
> *We use the _____ simple after* when *to talk about the future.*

 12

7 Practice

a Put the verbs in the right form. Use the future with *'ll/won't* or the present simple.

1 When Mary *finishes* (finish) work tonight, she *'ll do* (do) her shopping.
2 When Mary _____ (arrive) at the office tomorrow, she _____ (check) her messages.
3 She _____ (use) a different name when she _____ (go) abroad next week.
4 When she _____ (be) away next week, her family _____ (not be able to) contact her.
5 Her parents _____ (phone) her when she _____ (come) back next Sunday.
6 She _____ (probably write) a book when she _____ (retire).

b **Test a friend** Think of a question beginning *What will you do when ...?*, then ask a friend.

> What will you do when you get home after school?

> When I get home, I'll probably listen to some music.

8 Speaking *Your future*

Use what you know

Read the questions and think about your answers.

What will you do when you leave school?
What will you have to do / be able to do when you leave home?
What sort of things will be different when you get a job?

Then work with a friend and tell him/her your ideas about the future.

> I might get a job, or I may go to university.

> When I leave home, I'll have to cook my own meals.

In Step 2 you study
- verbs and nouns that go together
- *should*
- second conditional
- responding to opinions

so that you can
- talk about what's right and wrong
- talk about hypothetical situations

1 Key vocabulary
Verbs and nouns that go together

a ⏱ Match the verbs in the box with the nouns. You've got two minutes!

make	break	tell	keep

1 – a promise / – a mistake
2 – the truth / – lies
3 – a promise / – a secret
4 – a promise / – the law

🔊 Listen and check.

b Complete the sentences with words from 1a.

1 When you _____ a promise, you should try to _____ it.
2 We all _____ mistakes. It's normal!
3 I think you should always tell the _____ .
4 You shouldn't _____ the law. You can't always do what you want.
5 I don't believe everything that Mark says. He often tells _____ .
6 Don't tell Lucy. She can never _____ a secret.
7 If you break your _____ , I'll never speak to you again!

Remember!
You **should** be honest.
You **shouldn't** tell lies.
We use should/shouldn't + verb *to give advice or to express an opinion about what's right or wrong.*

2 Presentation *What would you do?*

a 🔊 Listen to the questionnaire and follow in your book. Have you ever been in any of these situations?

How honest are you?

1 If you found a friend's diary, what would you do?
 a I'd give it back. I wouldn't read it.
 b I'd read it and then tell my friend.
 c I'd probably have a quick look, but I wouldn't admit it.
2 If someone asked you for advice, would you:
 a give him/her your honest opinion?
 b tell your friend that he/she must decide?
 c say something nice, even if it wasn't true?
3 If a shop assistant gave you too much change, would you give it back?
 a Yes, I probably would.
 b I would if it was a lot of money.
 c No, I wouldn't. I'd keep the money and leave the shop quickly.

b Read the questionnaire again and choose your answers. Then check your score.

3 Key grammar *Second conditional*
Read the examples and complete the explanation.

If I **found** someone's diary, I**'d read** it.
If I **looked** at someone's diary, I **wouldn't admit** it.
If you **found** a friend's diary, **would** you **read** it?
Yes, I **would**. / No, I **wouldn't**.

We use the second conditional when we imagine a hypothetical situation in the present or the future.

We form the second conditional with If + _____ s*imple and* _____/wouldn't + verb.

G 14

4 Would you tell a lie to help a close friend?
  a No, I wouldn't. It's wrong to tell lies.
  b I might. It would depend on the situation.
  c Yes, I would. You should always support your friends.

5 What would you do if the person next to you copied your answers in an exam?
  a I'd talk to him/her about it afterwards.
  b I don't know. I might ask my parents for their advice.
  c I probably wouldn't do anything.

Mostly 'a's: You're super-honest – if you answered all the questions honestly!

Mostly 'b's: You're not always sure what to do, but you usually think about things carefully.

Mostly 'c's: It's true that no one's perfect, but are you someone that your friends can trust?

4 Practice

a Complete the sentences. Use the right form of the verb.

  1 If I _found_ (find) someone's wallet, I _'d probably take_ (probably take) it to the police station.
  2 If I _____ (know) the answer, I _____ (not tell) you!
  3 If a friend _____ (do) something wrong, _____ (you/tell) anyone?
  4 I _____ (be) really surprised if Danny _____ (break) his promise. He's a very loyal person.
  5 If you _____ (not be) so secretive, perhaps we _____ (be able to) help you.
  6 What _____ (you/do) if someone _____ (have) a heart attack?
  7 If you _____ (not shout) so loudly, people _____ (not get) so angry with you!
  8 If you _____ (have to) speak in front of hundreds of people, _____ (you/feel) nervous?

b **What about you?** If you could invite a famous person to dinner, who would you choose? Make sentences with:

I'd choose …   I'd wear …   We'd have … for dinner. We'd talk about …

Then work with a friend and compare your ideas.

5 Listening   *A discussion on the radio*

a 🔊 Listen to a discussion on the radio. Which question from the questionnaire are they talking about?

b 🔊 Look at the words in the box and sentences 1–4. Then listen again. Choose the right words and complete the sentences.

> keep   honest   dishonest   honesty
> give it back   break the law

  1 Peter thinks that _____ is very important.
  2 Jill believes that everyone is _____ sometimes.
  3 If someone gave Peter too much change, he'd _____ .
  4 Jill would probably _____ the money if she was in a big department store.

c 🔊 Now listen to the next part of the programme and complete the survey results.

In a recent survey of young people, _____% said they might keep the money if they were in a department store. Only _____% would keep it if they were in a local shop.

6 Key expressions   *Responding to opinions*

Look at these expressions from the discussion in Exercise 5. How would you say them in your language?

I know what you mean, but …
I agree. / I don't agree.
That's true, but …   Yes, exactly!

7 Speaking   *What do you think?*

Use what you know

Choose at least two questions from the questionnaire and talk about the answers with your friends.

> I'd tell a lie to help a friend. I think that's OK.

> I don't agree. You shouldn't be dishonest.

In Step 3 you
- read an article about a 'con man'
- study *because, so*

so that you can
- write an imaginary 'sales talk'

1 Share your ideas *Tourist attractions*

What do you know about the places and monuments in the photos? Where are they? What are the most popular tourist attractions in your country?

> One of the most famous buildings in Spain is the Alhambra Palace.

2 Reading

a Reading skills *Predicting the topic of a text*
Look at the picture and the title of the text. What do you think it might be about?

b Read the text about a 'con man' called Arthur Ferguson. What did he try to do? Were your predictions correct?

For sale?

One morning in 1923, a Scottish actor called Arthur Ferguson was standing in Trafalgar Square in London when he saw a rich American tourist and suddenly had an idea. The tourist was admiring Nelson's Column, so Ferguson pretended to be the official guide to the square. He told the American all about the history of the statue, the lions and the fountains. Then he said that, unfortunately, the British Government had to sell them, because they needed the money.

Ferguson was a very good liar, so his first 'customer' believed him completely. He asked the price. 'Thirty thousand dollars,' Ferguson replied. The delighted tourist immediately wrote a cheque. Ferguson gave him a receipt and the name and address of the company that would move Nelson's Column to America for him. Then he disappeared.

Later that summer, Ferguson sold Big Ben, the famous clock, to another American tourist. His third 'customer' gave him a deposit of $10,000 for the home of the Royal Family, Buckingham Palace.

In 1925, Ferguson decided to emigrate to the United States to continue his successful new career. He went to Washington DC. There he sold the White House to a visitor from Texas, who gave him a deposit of $100,000.

After that, he moved to New York, where he tried to sell the Statue of Liberty to an Australian tourist. 'It would look wonderful in Sydney Harbour!' he said. But the Australian went to the police. Finally, Ferguson was caught and he spent the next five years in prison.

c **Comprehension check**

🔊 Listen, and read the text again. Are these sentences true or false?

1 Arthur Ferguson worked in Trafalgar Square. He was the official guide.
2 The British Government wanted to sell Nelson's Column.
3 The American tourist wanted to buy Nelson's Column, so he gave Ferguson a cheque.
4 Ferguson didn't really move Nelson's Column to the USA.
5 Ferguson was successful because people thought he was telling the truth.
6 One of his customers went to live in Buckingham Palace.
7 A visitor from Texas wanted to buy the White House.
8 After that, Ferguson went to Sydney, Australia.

3 Word work because, so

Look at the examples. Then join the pairs of sentences. Use *because* or *so*.

He was a good liar, **so** everyone believed him.
They believed him **because** he was a good liar.

1 He went to prison. He broke the law.
2 He broke the law. He went to prison.
3 The American really wanted Nelson's Column. He wrote a cheque immediately.
4 No one trusts Vince. He can't keep a secret.
5 They knew Ferguson was lying. They went to the police.
6 I sometimes pretend that I agree. I don't like arguing.

Writing guide *'Sales talk'!*

● Give details about the place you're selling.

It's the most beautiful ... in the country!
It was built in ...
The views are fantastic.

● Say why you think it would be a 'good buy'. Use the second conditional.

If you bought it, you'd live like a king!
You'd be able to have some fantastic parties.

● Give the price.

You can have it for $800,000. A bargain!

4 Writing *An imaginary sale!*

Use what you know

Think of a famous place or monument in your country and imagine you're trying to sell it to a rich tourist. What would you say? Write your ideas.

Extra exercises

1 Complete the sentences. Use *might/may* or *might not/may not* and these verbs.

> remember   go   find   have   keep   look after

1 I'll try to finish this tonight but I _____ enough time.
2 Don't do that! If you break the law, you _____ to prison.
3 Steve has promised to help me, but he _____ his promise.
4 Ellie _____ . She hasn't got a very good memory.
5 Our neighbours _____ our dog while we're on holiday. I hope so.
6 My mum's looking for a holiday house. She _____ one in the south of France.

2 Match 1–6 with a–f and make six sentences.

1 Sandra will probably visit her sister in New Zealand
2 We're going to look after our grandparents' house
3 I might ask Dad for some advice
4 I promise I'll go to bed
5 You'll be able to drive
6 I'll go and see Buckingham Palace

a when this programme ends.
b when you're 17.
c when I visit London.
d when she leaves school.
e when he gets home.
f when they're away.

3 Complete the sentences. Use the second conditional.

1 If we _____ a boat, we _____ go sailing in the Mediterranean. (*own, can*)
2 I _____ nervous if I _____ appear on television. (*feel, have to*)
3 If you _____ to Paul, he _____ so angry. (*apologise, not be*)
4 If we _____ wars, the world _____ a much better place. (*not have, be*)
5 More people _____ to that café if they _____ nicer food. (*go, serve*)
6 I _____ to the leisure centre if it _____ a swimming pool. (*not go, not have*)

4 Write the questions using the second conditional.

1 *Would you miss me if I moved to a different school?*

1 A: you miss me / if / I move to a different school?
  B: Yes, of course I would.
2 A: I look good / if / I wear a lot of make-up?
  B: No, you wouldn't.
3 A: What / you do / if / you win £1,000?
  B: I'd buy a new computer.
4 A: If / you go abroad, / where you go?
  B: I'd travel all round the world.
5 A: your parents worry / if / you not contact them?
  B: Yes, they would.

5 Read the conversation and choose the right word(s) for each space.

A: Where's Matt? He promised to meet me here this afternoon.
B: You shouldn't believe Matt. He often tells ¹_____ and he often ²_____ his promises.
A: I ³_____ agree. I know he sometimes forgets things, but he isn't dishonest. And if I had a problem, I'd always ask Matt for advice.
B: Well, I wouldn't. When Joanne told him about her boyfriend, everyone in the school heard about it. He can't ⁴_____ a secret.
A: We all ⁵_____ mistakes.
B: ⁶_____ , but with Matt these things happen all the time. I don't trust him.

1 a the truth	b lies	c secrets
2 a breaks	b makes	c keeps
3 a don't	b won't	c may not
4 a keep	b break	c tell
5 a have	b do	c make
6 a I don't know	b That's true	c Yes, exactly

6 How do you say these sentences in your language?

1 I'm afraid I can't tell you.
2 You shouldn't tell lies.
3 She can't keep a secret.
4 Don't forget to give it back.
5 I know what you mean, but I don't agree.
6 Yes, exactly!

Extra reading

The code talkers

Do codes interest you or irritate you?
What sort of codes do we use in everyday life?

For more than a hundred years, white Americans taught Native American Indians to speak English. A member of the Navajo tribe, now in his 80s, says: 'We were told, "Don't speak Navajo", and they used to wash our mouths with soap!'

Then, during World War II, all that changed. The United States army realised that if they used the Navajo language to send radio messages, it would be an excellent, safe code. It did not exist in writing and only the Navajo Indians could speak it. So a group of them were invited to join the army and they became 'code talkers'. They worked as radio operators so that the Americans could communicate in secret, knowing that the enemy would not be able to break their code.

A lot of common military words did not exist in Navajo so, for example, *da-he-ti-hi*, the Navajo word for 'bird', became the code word for 'aeroplane' and *besh lo*, meaning 'iron fish', was the code for 'submarine'. For names of people and places, the code talkers used code words for each letter of the alphabet: for example, the word *be-la-sana* meant 'apple', so it represented the letter *a*.

The code was a secret for many years after the war because the USA did not know if they might need to use it again one day. The code talkers could not talk about their work and their heroism was forgotten. Finally, on July 26th 2001, five elderly Native Americans received the Congressional Gold Medal – one of the USA's highest awards. They were the last survivors from a group of men who helped to change the course of history.

ABOUT GENETIC CODES

The most complex code of all is the one inside our bodies: the DNA (deoxyribonucleic acid) in our 50,000 trillion cells is the 'building plan' for all life. Believe it or not, 30% of a human's DNA is the same as the DNA of a lettuce!

Task

Read the text at least once. How did the code talkers represent people and places? Work with a friend and use the code to make a sentence from these words.

Meet ...

MONEY**E**XAM**E**ARLY**T**OASTMAKEEASY
APPLETENMAGICICEDARKNICEINGO
HATTRUEUSNOTDAYEGGROADTALK
HELPEYEBAGRUNITDATEGAMEEAR

Grammar check

1 The future with *will* and *going to*
Work it out for yourself

> **Read the dialogue and explanations 1–4, then match each explanation with *will/won't* or *going to*.**
>
> MR BOYD: *I'm going to clean the house on Saturday morning. Can anyone help me?*
> MRS BOYD: *You must ALL help Dad. I **won't be able** to help him.*
> FIONA: *Sorry, Dad. There's a party on Friday night. I expect it**'ll finish** really late.*
>   *So I'll probably **be** in bed on Saturday morning.*
> SALLY: *Sorry, Dad. I'm going to spend the weekend at Kate's. We're going to paint her bedroom.*
> PAUL: *Don't worry, Dad. I'll **help** you, and I **won't get up** late, honestly.*
>
> 1 Mr Boyd and Sally talk about their intentions. They've already made plans for Saturday morning.
> 2 Paul makes a decision at the moment of speaking. He makes an offer and a promise.
> 3 Fiona makes a prediction about Saturday morning.
> 4 Mrs Boyd talks about a future fact.

Check that you can

● use *will* and *going to*.

Complete the sentences.
Use '*ll (will)/won't* or *be going to*.

1 It's my birthday on Friday. I _'ll_ be 17.
2 I haven't got any plans for the weekend. I _____ probably stay at home.
3 Have you heard the news? They _____ build a new gym at school.
4 Jack has gone to Paris for a week, so he _____ be at school tomorrow.
5 Give me that suitcase. I _____ carry it for you.
6 Alex is studying medicine. He _____ be a doctor.
7 A: Have you got any plans for tonight?
    B: Yes. I _____ watch the match on TV.
8 A: Can you come tomorrow?
    B: I'm not sure. I _____ phone you tonight.

2 *when* in future sentences
Work it out for yourself

> **Look at the picture, then answer the questions and complete the explanation.**
>
> EMMA: **When I get** home, I'll have a hot shower.
>
> 1 Is Emma thinking about the present or the future?
> 2 Is the verb *get* in the present or the future form?
>
> In future sentences, we use a verb in the _____ after *when*.

Check that you can

● use *when* in future sentences.

Complete the sentences with *will* or the present simple of the verb.

1 I _'ll be_ (be) 18 when I _leave_ (leave) school.
2 I think I _____ (live) abroad when I _____ (be) older.
3 When my sister _____ (come) back from Australia, we _____ (have) a big celebration.
4 I _____ (phone) you when I _____ (get) to the station.
5 I _____ (put) the candles on the cake when it _____ (be) ready.
6 They _____ (buy) some fireworks when the shop _____ (open).

3 The first and second conditional

Work it out for yourself

First conditional (*If* + present simple + *will/won't*)	Second conditional (*If* + past simple + *would/wouldn't*)

1 *If* it **rains** this afternoon, Amy **will be** angry.	2 *If* it **rained** this afternoon, Fabio **would be** pleased.

A Look at the pictures and sentences 1 and 2, then answer these questions.

   1 Is it possible that it will rain at Amy's tennis match?

   2 Do you think it will rain at Fabio's farm?

B Match sentences 1 and 2 with these explanations.

   a It's a hypothetical situation. It's perhaps impossible.

   b It's a real possibility.

C Read these sentences and complete the explanation.

*Fabio's plants won't grow **unless** it rains soon. = Fabio's plants won't grow **if it doesn't rain** soon.*

We can use .... + a verb in the affirmative. It usually means the same as .... + a verb in the negative.

Check that you can

3.1 ● use the first conditional.

Complete the sentences. Use *if/unless* and the right form of the verb.

1 The ice cream _will melt_ (*melt*) _if_ you .... (*leave*) it in the sun.

2 .... you .... (*break*) your promise, I .... (*be*) angry.

3 You .... (*not pass*) your piano exam .... you .... (*practise*) every day.

4 .... we .... (*not leave*) now, we .... (*miss*) the bus.

3.2 ● use the second conditional.

Make sentences using *if* and the second conditional.

1 *If Kate spoke more slowly, people would understand her.*

1 Kate speaks too quickly. People don't understand her.

2 Gran hasn't got a dog. She's lonely.

3 I'm not good at football. I don't play in the school team.

4 Ben is so stupid. He spends all his money on expensive clothes.

5 Davina tells lies. People don't listen to her.

4 *might* and *may*

Work it out for yourself

Read the conversations, then answer the questions.

TANYA: *Shall we join the queue?*

JOE: *Hang on a minute. We **may/might** be here for hours.*

DAN: *Do you think my sister will like this one?*

EMMA: *Er … she **may not/might not** like the colours.*

1 Are Joe and Emma talking about the present or the future?

2 Are they certain or uncertain?

3 Which two verbs do we use to describe future possibilities?

Check that you can

● use *may* and *might*.

Complete the dialogues. Use *may/might, may not/might not*.

1 A: Will you see Frank today?

   B: I _might_ see him after school. I'm not sure.

2 A: I .... see you tomorrow.

   B: Oh, why not?

3 A: I .... pass the exam.

   B: Stop worrying! You .... get some easy questions.

4 A: Someone .... steal our bikes.

   B: I hope not. That would be terrible.

5 A: I'll see you in town at eight o'clock.

   B: I .... come. I've got a headache.

Vocabulary and expressions

Special occasions
Congratulations!
Good luck!
Happy anniversary
Happy birthday
Happy New Year

cake
candle
(to) celebrate
celebration
costume
decorations
fireworks
guest
present
procession

Expressions
I guess so.
I guess not.
I hope so.
I hope not.

Invitations and replies
afterwards
(to) come over
fancy dress
I'd love to come.
I'm afraid I won't be able to come.
Let me know.
note
outdoors
reception
(to) reply
... requests the pleasure of your company
RSVP
(to) welcome

Verbs with *look*
(to) look after
(to) look at
(to) look for
(to) look forward to
(to) look round
(to) look up

Verbs and nouns that go together
(to) break a promise
(to) break the law
(to) keep a promise
(to) keep a secret
(to) make a mistake
(to) make a promise
(to) tell lies
(to) tell the truth

Responding to opinions
I agree. / I don't agree.
I know what you mean, but ...
That's true but ...
Yes, exactly!

'Sales talk'
(to) admire
career
cheque
'con man'
delighted
deposit (n.)
fountain
harbour
liar
monument
official
receipt
tourist attraction
unfortunately

Study skills 4
Preparing for tests and exams

🕐 When you've got a test or an exam, how many of the following do you do? For each item, score 2 points if it's something you usually do, 1 point if it's something you sometimes do, and 0 if it's something you never do. You've got three minutes!

1 Make sure you know what you'll have to do in the exam.
2 Make a revision timetable.
3 Revise regularly for several weeks before your exam.
4 Remember to practise reading, writing, listening and speaking in English.
5 Look at past tests and exams, and try to do one or two of them.
6 Revise with a friend and test each other.
7 Revise in a quiet place and not in front of the TV!
8 If you want your brain to work well, drink plenty of water and get plenty of sleep!

Add up your score. If it's under 7, then choose at least one thing that you should or shouldn't do in the future!

I shouldn't try to revise while I'm watching TV.

How's it going?

● **Your rating**

Look again at pages 88 and 89. For each section decide on your rating: Good ✓ ✓ ✓   Not bad ✓ ✓   I can't remember much ✓

● **Vocabulary**

Look at the Vocabulary list for one minute. Then work with a friend. Can he/she remember at least one word or phrase for each topic?

● **Test a friend**

Look again at Units 7 and 8. Think of at least two questions, then ask a friend.

What's Mary Martin's job?

Where did Beth and Andy get married?

● **Correcting mistakes**

Can you correct these mistakes? In some sentences, there is more than one mistake.

1 I'll ring you when I'll arrive to the airport.
2 If I had more money, I'll buy a new computer.
3 'Will you can come tomorrow?' 'I hope that yes.'
4 Our friends have got a new dog. They'll call him Romeo.
5 I'm agree with you. People shouldn't to break their promises.

● **Your Workbook**

Complete the Learning Diaries for Units 7 and 8.

Coursework 4 *Our school magazine*

Read the letters in this month's edition of *Pulse*. Then think of a topic that interests you and write a letter for a magazine page.

Letters to the editor

If you've got something to say, then why not write? Send your letters to: The Editors, *Pulse* Magazine, Greenside Community College, Greenside Road, Liverpool LP3 9OB.
email: pulsemag@greenside.net

Our school uniform

Dear Editors,
I hate wearing a school uniform and so do all my friends. If we didn't have to wear a uniform, we'd be much happier and we might even work better too. School uniform is old-fashioned and unnecessary. If you agree, please write to me – or to the Letters page at *Pulse*.

Steve Corder   Year 9

stevethewonderboy@supermail.com
PS *Pulse* is a great magazine. Thanks!

Crazy?

Dear *Pulse*,
Why do footballers and actors get paid millions of pounds when my mum, who is a nurse, gets paid very little? It seems crazy to me. Do they deserve all that money? Do they need it? Of course they don't!

Mia McGee   Year 11

TV violence

Dear Editors,
Adults often say there's too much violence on TV and in computer games, for example *Streetfighter*. But, in my opinion, it's not true that young people think violence is normal because we see it on our screens. I hate violence.

The news on TV is often as violent as computer games but my parents don't mind when I watch that. What do other *Pulse* readers think?

Ollie Cook   Year 8

In fashion

Dear *Pulse*,
Your article 'Slaves to fashion?' was excellent. I don't think it's important to follow the latest fashion. I choose clothes that I like, and I don't care if they're 'trendy' or not. We shouldn't worry about our appearance so much.

Helen Redwood   Year 10

Mrs Massey

We want to say a big THANK YOU to Mrs Massey, who is leaving at the end of the term. She has been our history teacher for three years and we all think she's brilliant.

Mrs Massey, you're one in a million! Thanks for everything. We wish you all the very best.

Year 11 History Group

Rock Against Famine

Dear *Pulse*,
Our 'Rock Against Famine' concert raised more than £800. Congratulations to everyone who took part.

Annie Howard (Head of Music)

Module 5

Living together

In Module 5 Steps 1 and 2 you study

Grammar

- Verb/preposition + -ing form
- -ing form and to + verb
- want/ask/tell someone to do something
- Expressions of quantity
- Question words
- Subject and object questions

Vocabulary

- People in groups
- Food

Expressions

- Requests and responses
- Expressing preferences

so that you can

- Talk about being in a group
- Describe your likes and dislikes and interview a friend
- Ask people to do things
- Make and respond to polite requests
- Talk about things you'd like to change
- Ask and answer different types of question
- Do a general knowledge quiz

Life and culture

Romeo and Juliet
Make Poverty History

Coursework 5

Part 5 The ads page
You make adverts to put in your school magazine.

In Step 3 you ...

read

- A TV commentary
- A review of a book

study

- too + adjective; adjective + enough
- Adjectives ending in -ed/-ing
- Using pronouns and possessive adjectives
- Recognising facts and opinions

so that you can

- Write a description of teenagers in your country
- Write a review

What's it about?

What can you say about the pictures?

Now match the pictures with sentences 1–5.

1 Who calls their city *The Big Apple*?
2 They eat parasites which are bad for crocodiles.
3 I want you all to say 'cheese'.
4 I like working in a team.
5 We import more and more food.

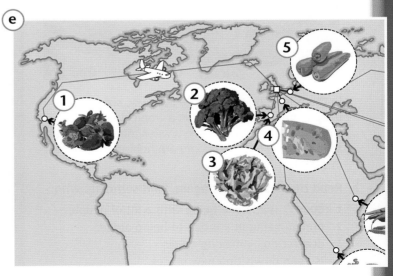

9 Groups

In Step 1 you study
- names of different groups
- verb/preposition + -ing form

so that you can
- talk about being in a group
- describe yourself and interview a friend

1 Key vocabulary *People in groups*

a ⏱ Match the words with the photos 1–8. You've got two minutes!

> audience   band   choir   club   crowd
> gang   orchestra   team

🔊 Listen and check.

b **What about you?** Do you belong to any groups?

> I'm in a band at school. I joined it last year.

2 Presentation *I'm good at making things*

a 🔊 Listen and follow the text in your book. Find at least one sentence which is true for you.

In the television programme *Survivor*, sixteen people are chosen to live on a tropical island. They work in two teams but, every week, one person has to leave. These three people are hoping to take part in *Survivor*.

b Read the descriptions again. Find someone who:
1. doesn't really like being with a lot of people.
2. prefers being in a group to being alone.
3. doesn't enjoy making meals.
4. is keen on visiting new places.
5. likes staying in bed in the morning.
6. isn't good at speaking Spanish.

c Imagine you're on *Survivor*. Choose one of the three people for your team. Compare your ideas.

> I'd choose Laura Gordon, because she's good at solving problems.

	Melanie Knight
Do you prefer doing things on your own or in a group?	I prefer doing things in a group. I don't really like being on my own.
Is there anything that you really like or dislike?	I'm quite keen on playing team games. I hate getting up early.
What are your strengths and weaknesses?	I'm a good leader and I don't mind making difficult decisions. Talking too much is my biggest weakness.
Why do you want to be on *Survivor*?	I'd like to live on a tropical island!

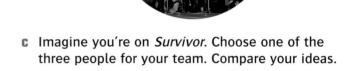

3 Key grammar

Verb/preposition + -ing *form*

Complete the examples and read the explanations.

> She **likes** work**ing** in a team.
> She **can't stand** cook_____ .
> I **don't mind** do_____ things on my own.
>
> *Verbs describing likes and dislikes are often followed by a verb +* -ing.
>
> I'm good **at** solv**ing** problems.
> He's keen **on** play**ing** team games.
>
> *We use the* -ing *form after prepositions.*

G ➔ 25a-b, 26

Remember!

I **like being** on TV.
I'**d like to be** an actor.
Do you **want to be** on Survivor?

We use to *+ verb after* want, would like, would love, would hate.

Rob Green	**Laura Gordon**
I'm an independent person. I'm not very keen on being with a lot of people.	I like working in a team, but I don't mind doing things on my own.
I'm interested in travelling and I love being outdoors. I can't stand people who tell silly jokes.	I enjoy running. I can't stand cooking, and I hate insects.
Strengths? Well, I'm a carpenter so I'm good at making things. And weaknesses? I'm useless at foreign languages.	I'm good at solving problems. But I've got a very loud laugh that sometimes annoys people!
I think I've got a lot of skills that would be useful on the island.	I want to be an actor, so I'd love to be on TV.

4 Practice

a Describe these people using the underlined verbs and a verb + -ing. Write one sentence each time.

1 *Melanie loves being on television.*

1 Melanie is on television. She <u>loves</u> it.
2 Luke shares a room with his brother. He <u>doesn't like</u> it.
3 Laura sings in her local choir. She really <u>enjoys</u> it.
4 Danny usually does the washing up, but he <u>hates</u> it.
5 Karim doesn't often go in lifts. He <u>can't stand</u> them.
6 Mary often works at the weekend, but she <u>doesn't mind</u> that.
7 I usually sit at the back of the class. I <u>prefer</u> it.

b Make sentences with the -ing form of these verbs.

keep cook find listen help paint

1 Thanks very much for <u>*helping*</u> me.
2 Don't ask Clare to make the dinner. She's useless at _____ .
3 Do you ever worry about _____ a job when you leave school?
4 Laura's very keen on _____ . She won an art competition last year.
5 I like talking to Luke, but he isn't very good at _____ secrets.
6 Rob's quite selfish. He isn't interested in _____ to his friends' problems.

c **Test a friend** Write a description of someone in the class using at least one verb + -ing. Can your friend guess who it is?

> He likes collecting things and he's good at organising parties.

> Is it Pablo?

5 Key pronunciation /ŋ/ /n/

🔊 **Listen and repeat the words.**

1 /ŋ/ song ring helping cooking
2 /n/ person chicken begin women

🔊 **Listen and practise this sentence.**

We go surfing, swimming and diving in the Indian Ocean.

6 Writing and speaking *An interview for* Survivor

Use what you know

Look at the questions in the *Survivor* questionnaire and write your own answers. Then work with a friend and ask each other the questions. Would you and your friend get on well if you were on *Survivor* together?

In Step 2 you study
- *want/ask/tell someone to do something*
- requests and responses

so that you can
- ask people to do things
- make and respond to polite requests

1 Share your ideas

What do you say in your language when you ask someone to do something for you? Do you use different language when you speak to an adult and when you speak to someone of your own age?

> I'm more polite when I speak to an adult!

2 Presentation *I want you to say 'cheese'!*

a What can you say about the photos?

b 🔊 Close your book and listen to the conversation. What does everyone say when Luke takes the photo? Can you guess why?

Luke's class is on a school trip. They're going to go on the ferry across the River Mersey. Luke wants to take a photo.

LUKE: I want to take a photo of everyone. Nadia, can you tell the others to come over here?

NADIA: Yes, OK.

LUKE: Mr Marshall, would you stand in the middle, please?

MR MARSHALL: Yes, sure.

DANNY: Do you want us to say 'cheese'?

LUKE: In a minute. Mr Marshall, I can't see John. Would you mind moving to the left a bit?

MR MARSHALL: No, of course not. No problem.

LUKE: Thanks. Clare, could you stand a bit closer to Nadia?

DANNY: Hurry up, Luke. This is taking ages!

LUKE: All right. I know! Clare, I asked you to stand closer to Nadia.

CLARE: Sorry, Luke. Is this all right?

LUKE: Yes, that's fine. Look at me, everyone, and don't move!

DANNY: Do you want us to wave?

LUKE: No! ... Right. I want you all to say 'cheese'. One, two, three ...

EVERYONE: Cheese!

c 🔊 Listen again and follow in your book. Match 1–6 with a–f and make six sentences about the conversation.

1	Luke asks Mr Marshall to stand	a	to stand closer to Nadia.
2	He asks him to	b	them to say 'cheese'.
3	Luke wants Clare	c	move to the left.
4	Danny tells	d	wave.
5	Luke doesn't want his friends to	e	in the middle.
6	Luke wants	f	Luke to hurry up.

3 Key grammar want/ask/tell someone to do something

Complete the examples and read the explanation.

> Luke **asks** Mr Marshall **to** stand in the middle.
> He **asks** him .... move.
> He **wants** .... **to** stand closer to Nadia.
> He **tells** everyone **to** .... 'cheese'.
>
> *Be careful of the word order:*
> want/ask/tell + *noun/object pronoun* + to + *verb*.

G ➤ 23

4 Practice

Put the words in the right order and make eight sentences.

1 Nadia wants me to take a photo.

1 Nadia (a / wants / to / photo / take / me)
2 Mr Marshall (coach / get on / wants / to / us / the)
3 He (to / students / the / told / hurry up)
4 I (you / asked / me / to / help)
5 John (me / asked / to / his / band / join)
6 He (be / wants / singer / to / me / the)
7 They (drums / Ben / play / to / the / want)
8 They (come / Saturday / told / him / to / on)

5 Key expressions *Requests and responses*

a Match the requests with the pictures.

Could you tell me the way to the post office?
Would you take the dog for a walk?
Would you mind opening the door for me?
Can you lend me your CD player?

b Work in pairs. Choose the right response and make dialogues.

1 Yes, of course. It's over there.
2 I guess so. But be careful with it!
3 No, of course not. No problem.
4 I'm afraid I can't. Sorry, but I'm going to Pete's.

6 Listening *Could you help?*

a [cassette] Close your books and listen. How many different people do you hear?

b [cassette] Listen again, then answer these questions.

1 What does Mr Marshall want Danny to do?
2 Does Danny say yes or no? Why?
3 What does Karim ask Danny to do?
4 What does Danny say?
5 What does Lorina want him to do?
6 Can Danny help her?
7 Why is Danny's mum annoyed?

7 Speaking
A telephone conversation

Use what you know

Work with a friend. You want your friend to do something for you. Act a telephone conversation like the ones in Exercise 6.

> Hi, it's Felix here. I'm going camping at the weekend. Could you lend me your ...?

In Step 3 you
● read a TV commentary
● study *too* + adjective; adjective + *enough*

so that you can
● write a description of teenagers in your country

1 Share your ideas *Wildlife*

Are wildlife programmes popular in your country? Do you ever watch them? Can you remember any interesting facts that you've learnt from a wildlife programme?

> When a panda is born, it's smaller than a mouse.

2 Reading

a You're going to read part of a commentary from a TV programme about wildlife. Read the text once and then complete the captions with the photos.

Working together

❝ In tonight's programme we're going to look at how animals live and work together in different types of relationships.

Living in groups is normal for many animals, including humans. Some animals have amazing social systems. Ants, for example, live in huge nests. They work closely together and can communicate with each other. Each ant has a certain job to do. Only one, the queen, produces eggs, and worker ants look after them. Other workers bring food to the nest and soldier ants defend it. This system is incredibly successful. Ants have lived on Earth for at least 100 million years (much longer than humans) – and for every human, there are a million ants.

Sometimes animals from different species work together and help each other. A fascinating example is the relationship between Nile crocodiles and a bird called the Egyptian plover. Very few small animals are brave enough to go near a crocodile. Its huge jaws and sharp teeth are much too dangerous. But plovers walk inside a crocodile's open mouth! They aren't in danger because they eat parasites which are bad for crocodiles. In return, they get food and protection.

For many wild animals, humans are their greatest enemy – but some wild animals have learnt to live very comfortably beside us. In the UK foxes have moved into our cities. They live in our gardens and they get their food from our rubbish. In parts of North America wild bears come into town at night to find food. Rats are even happier in a human environment. They live in large numbers in our buildings and under our streets. Experts believe that there are at least 250,000 of them living in New York. ❞

1 _____ work together to collect food and protect their nest.

2

The _____ plover eats parasites inside a _____'s mouth.

b Comprehension check

🔊 **Listen, and read the text again. Then match 1–6 with a–f and make six sentences.**

1	Nile crocodiles	a	often make their homes in people's gardens.
2	Ants	b	like living in buildings.
3	Queen ants	c	have parasites in their mouths.
4	Foxes	d	are very good at working together.
5	Rats	e	aren't afraid of going near crocodiles.
6	Egyptian plovers	f	don't look after their eggs.

.... often live in towns and find their food in our ....

c Reading skills *Using pronouns and possessive adjectives*

Find these phrases and sentences in the text, and then read the words or sentences before them. What do the underlined words refer to?

1 them = eggs

1 ... worker ants look after <u>them</u>.
2 ... soldier ants defend <u>it</u>.
3 <u>Its</u> huge jaws and sharp teeth are much too dangerous.
4 <u>They</u> aren't in danger ...
5 ... they eat parasites <u>which</u> are bad for crocodiles.
6 ... some wild animals have learnt to live very comfortably beside <u>us</u>.
7 ... they get <u>their</u> food from our rubbish.
8 ... there are at least 250,000 of <u>them</u> living in New York.

3 Word work too *and* enough

Look at the examples.

They aren't **brave enough** to go near a crocodile.
Its huge jaws and sharp teeth are **too dangerous**.

Complete the sentences. Use the adjectives in the box with *too* or *enough*.

strong	deep	old
difficult	rich	expensive
small	careful	

1 I'm not going to buy those trainers. They're *too expensive* .
2 Gran can't carry that big bag! She isn't ....
3 Children shouldn't swim here. The water's ....
4 Not many people are .... to own a Porsche.
5 I can't do this maths problem. It's ....
6 I need a bigger rucksack. This one is ....
7 They can't get married. They aren't ....
8 He'll never be a good driver. He isn't ....

Writing guide *Writing a commentary*

- Introduce the topic of the programme.

  We've made a fascinating study of the behaviour of young humans in (your country).

- Make one or two general statements.

  Most teenagers are sociable animals.
  They usually spend a lot of time in groups.

- Give more detailed information.

  They usually wear ...
  They like eating ...
  When they're in a group, they often ...

4 Writing *A TV commentary*

Use what you know

Imagine you're making a 'wildlife programme' about teenagers! Write a short commentary. Think about these questions.

What do they wear / eat / talk about / do at the weekend?
What sort of things do they do at school?
How do they communicate?
Do they spend much time in groups?

Read your commentary to a friend.

Extra exercises

1 Choose the right words.

1 Angela enjoys _____ gymnastics.
   a do b doing c to do
2 I'm not coming to the match. I _____ stand watching football.
   a 'm not b don't c can't
3 Stuart's very keen _____ surfing.
   a on b at c for
4 I really want _____ this problem.
   a solve b to solve c solving
5 Thanks _____ me with my project.
   a to help b helping c for helping
6 A: Do you like soap operas?
   B: They're OK. I _____ watching them.
   a hate b prefer c don't mind

2 Read the text. Put the letters in the right order and make words describing groups of people.

I went to the Radley Concert Hall last night. My uncle was playing the violin in the ¹*thocarers* and my sister was singing in the ²*horic*. All the tickets were sold and there was a big ³*drocw* outside when we got there. I sat in the ⁴*enduciae* with Mum and Dad. It was a good concert, I suppose, but I'd really prefer to listen to a rock ⁵*dnab*. I'm not good at music like the rest of my family. My main interest is sport. I'm in the football ⁶*mate* at school, and my ambition is to play for one of the big city ⁷*bulsc*.

3 Write these sentences in a different way. Use the words in the box.

enjoy / learn
not keen on / use
useless at / dance
good at / act
can't stand / play
don't mind / eat

1 *I'm useless at dancing.*

1 I'm a very bad dancer.
2 Maria really hates basketball.
3 My brother likes foreign languages.
4 I think yoghurt is OK.
5 Robert acts very well.
6 Mum doesn't like computers much.

4 Write sentences using the words in brackets.

1 *She told him to tidy his room.*

1 Richard's mother was annoyed with him. (*she told / tidy his room*)
2 I left a message for Fiona. (*I asked / meet me at the library*)
3 Kate tried to ring you. (*she wanted / go to the gym with her*)
4 We saw Greg and Hannah at the bus stop. (*we asked / come to our place*)
5 My parents showed me a letter which was written in English. (*they wanted / translate it*)
6 Mrs Harrison gave us a lot of homework. (*she told / finish it for Friday*)

5 Read Mr Marshall's requests. For each one, write a question and answer using *want*.

1 *What does Mr Marshall want Hannah to do? He wants her to clean the board.*

1 'Hannah, can you clean the board, please?'
2 'Luke, could you close the door?'
3 'Nadia and Clare, would you stop talking, please?'
4 'Danny, would you mind reading the next paragraph?'
5 'Anna, would you give everyone a book?'

6 Complete the conversations. Use your imagination and think of requests at home or at school.

1 A: Excuse me, could you ¹_____ ?
   B: Yes, ²_____ .
   A: Thanks very much.
2 A: Would you mind ³_____ ?
   B: No, of course not. No problem.
3 A: I need some help. Can you ⁴_____ , please?
   B: I'm afraid ⁵_____ . Sorry, but ⁶_____ .

7 How do you say these sentences in your language?

1 I'm useless at cooking.
2 I can't stand being on my own.
3 She doesn't mind working at the weekend.
4 This is taking ages!
5 Would you mind moving to the left?
6 Would you take the dog for a walk?

Romeo and Juliet

Do you know the story of Romeo and Juliet? Who wrote the original play?

HE STORY OF ROMEO AND JULIET takes place in Verona, Italy. Two powerful families, the Capulets and the Montagues, have been enemies for years and there are frequent fights between them in the streets of the city. Juliet's parents, Lord and Lady Capulet, want their daughter to marry a wealthy young man called Paris. They hold a party, so that Juliet can meet him.

Romeo – a Montague – decides to go to the party. When he and Juliet meet, they immediately fall in love and they agree to get married as soon as possible. The next day Romeo goes to see his friend Friar Lawrence. The friar agrees to help them. Romeo and Juliet get married in secret.

But their happiness is soon destroyed. There is another fight and Mercutio, Romeo's friend, is killed by Tybalt, Juliet's cousin. Then, in a moment of anger, Romeo kills Tybalt. The Prince announces that Romeo must leave Verona for ever.

Juliet is desperate. She visits Friar Lawrence and asks him to help her. He gives her a drug and explains that she will sleep for a long time and everyone will think she is dead. The friar promises to send a message to Romeo, who will come and rescue her.

But Romeo doesn't receive Friar Lawrence's message. He hears that Juliet is dead and he is heartbroken. He buys a bottle of poison and goes to the tomb where Juliet's body is lying. He takes the poison. When Juliet wakes up, she finds her young husband dead beside her. In despair, she kills herself with his dagger.

When the Capulets and the Montagues find the bodies of their two children side by side, they agree to stop fighting and live together in peace.

ABOUT SHAKESPEARE

The English writer William Shakespeare (1564–1616) wrote at least 37 plays, including *Romeo and Juliet*. Many of them are still performed at theatres all over the world.

Task

Who do you think says these things?

1 'You want me to marry your daughter?'
2 'Juliet and I are in love. We want to get married.'
3 'Mercutio was my friend and you've killed him!'
4 'You must leave Verona and never come back.'
5 'I'll give you a drug. You'll appear to be dead.'
6 'I want you to take a message to Romeo.'
7 'I can't live without you, Romeo.'
8 'We must stop fighting and live in peace.'

10 Food for thought

STEP 1

In Step 1 you study
- food vocabulary
- expressions of quantity
- expressing preferences

so that you can
- talk about things you'd like to change

1 Key vocabulary *Food*

🕐 **Match the words with the pictures on the map. You've got two minutes!**

beans broccoli carrots cheese chicken lettuce peas prawns rice strawberries

📻 **Listen and check.**

2 Presentation *It doesn't make any sense*

a 📻 **Cover the text and look at the map. Listen to Clare's talk. Which food words do you hear?**

Every day, someone at Clare's school gives a short talk called 'Thought for today'. Today it's Clare. Her talk is about 'food miles'.

I'm going to talk to you about 'food miles' – that's the distance our food travels before we buy it. Last night I checked the things in our fridge. There was some broccoli from Spain – that's a journey of 950 miles – and some beans from Kenya, 5,000 miles away. I couldn't find any vegetables from the UK. There were some strawberries from the USA – a journey of about 7,000 miles, and there was some chicken from Thailand, which is 6,600 miles away. Add it up! It's a lot of miles – and a lot of fuel.

Today we import more and more food. There are more huge supermarkets and fewer markets and small food shops. It doesn't make any sense. Perhaps one day we'll eat no local food at all, and there'll be no local shops. I think most people would prefer to eat fresh food. It's better for you because it's got more vitamins. And I'd rather walk to a local market than sit in a traffic jam on the way to a supermarket. Fewer food miles means less fuel and less damage to the environment. That's my thought for today.

b 📻 **Listen again and follow in your book. Are these sentences true or false?**

1 There was a lot of local food in Clare's fridge.
2 There was no fruit.
3 We import less food now than in the past.
4 Clare thinks that people want to eat fresh food.
5 Clare would like to have more supermarkets and fewer local shops.
6 Planes use a lot of fuel and they're bad for the environment.

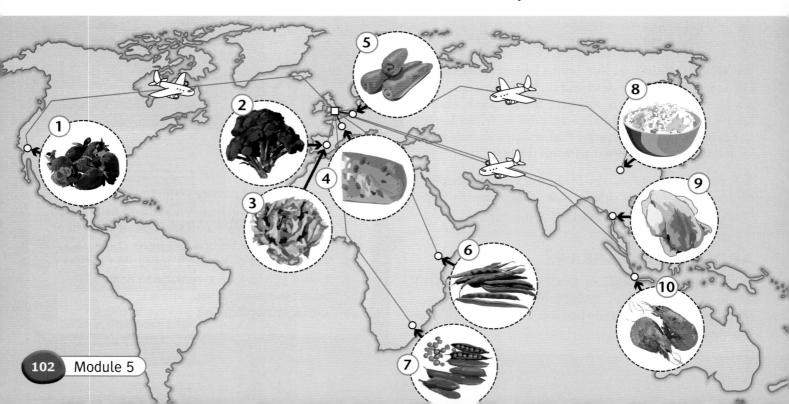

3 Key grammar *Expressions of quantity*

a Read the examples. Which nouns are countable and which are uncountable?

> There was **some** broccoli.
> There wasn't **any** broccoli.
> There were **some** vegetables.
> There weren't **any** vegetables.
> There's **a lot of** broccoli.
> There are **a lot of** vegetables.
>
> *We use* some, any *and* a lot of *with countable and uncountable nouns.*
>
> We won't eat **any** local food. = We'll eat **no** local food.
>
> *We use* any *with a verb in the negative. We use* no *with a verb in the affirmative.*

G ➤ 34

b Complete the explanation with *less, fewer, more*.

> **less** fuel / **fewer** shops
> **more** fuel / **more** shops
>
> *We use* .... *with uncountable nouns and* .... *with countable nouns.*
> *We use* .... *with uncountable and countable nouns.*

G ➤ 33

4 Practice

a For each word in the list, write *fewer, less, more, a lot of* or *no*. Make sentences which are true for you.

In my ideal world there would be …

no homework

homework   cars   love   traffic jams   free time
holidays   crime   freedom   wars   noise

If you have time, think of more examples.

b Complete the sentences with *any* or *no*.

1   I want to make a sandwich but we haven't got .... butter.
2   We've looked on the Internet but there isn't .... information about the concert.
3   I don't believe it! There's .... petrol in the car!
4   Ben isn't very healthy. He doesn't eat .... vegetables.
5   There's .... orange juice, I'm afraid. Would you like some apple juice?
6   Where are we going to sit? There are .... free seats.

c **Test a friend** Make another sentence for 4b. Can your friend complete the sentence?

I can't come to the cinema. I've got ..... money.

> **Try this!**
> Find the right vowels and make more food words.
>
> BR_ _D   H_M   F_SH   S_G_R   M_ _T
> S_LT   P_ST_   Y_GH_RT   S_ _P   C_R_ _L

5 Key pronunciation *Silent vowels*

 Listen and repeat these words. Can you find the 'silent' vowels?

1   strawberries ● ●
2   vegetables ● ● ●
3   chocolate ● ●
4   omelette ● ●

6 Key expressions
Expressing preferences

We'd prefer to eat fresh food.
I'd rather walk to the market.

a Work with a friend and practise the dialogue.
> A: Would you like to be a bird?
> B: No, I'd rather be a cat.

b Make questions using *Would you like to …* and these phrases. Make answers using *I'd rather …* or *I'd prefer to …* .

1   … go to the moon?
2   … play tennis tomorrow?
3   … have a scooter?
4   … watch the news?
5   … live on a tropical island?

7 Writing and speaking
My thought for today

> **Use what you know**
>
> Choose a topic from the list below and make at least three sentences describing your ideas.
>
> – a healthier life
> – a more interesting school
> – a better world
>
> **Use the expressions of quantity in Exercise 3.**
>
> *My ideas for a healthier life:*
> *Get more exercise.*
> *Eat fewer snacks.*

In Step 2 you study
● question words
● subject and object questions

so that you can
● ask and answer different types of question
● do a general knowledge quiz

1 Share your ideas

Look at the Remember! box and ask and answer at least three of the questions.

What's sushi?

I'm not sure. Is it fish?

If you have time, ask and answer more questions about food with *What, Where, When, How.*

Remember!

Question words

What's sushi?

Where does it come from?

When do you have your breakfast?

Who is the best cook in your family?

Why are oranges good for you?

Which pizza would you like – cheese and tomato or cheese and ham?

How do you make omelettes?

2 Presentation   *Who eats what?*

Read the questions and the answers. All the answers are in the wrong place. Match the questions with the right answers.

1 Which nationality drinks the most coffee?
a Coca-Cola
2 Which country do chips come from?
b London
3 What do frogs eat?
c Toast and cereal
4 What eats frogs?
d The Norwegians

Listen and check.

3 Key grammar   *Subject and object questions*

Read the examples and complete the explanations.

Subject questions

What eats frogs? — Snakes. (Snakes eat frogs.)
Who invented cornflakes? — W K Kellogg. (W K Kellogg invented cornflakes).

Object questions

What do snakes eat? — Frogs. (Snakes eat frogs.)
Which famous cereal did Kellogg invent? — Cornflakes. (Kellogg invented cornflakes.)

In the present simple and the past simple:
we use do/does/did *+ verb in* .... *questions.*
we don't use do/does/did *in* .... *questions.*

G ➔ 27

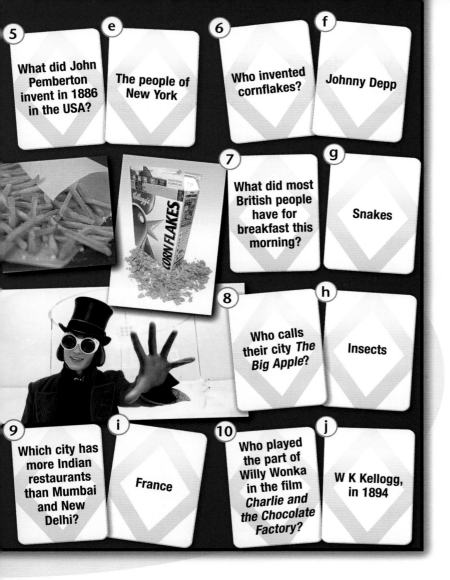

5
- What did John Pemberton invent in 1886 in the USA?
- **e** The people of New York
- **6** Who invented cornflakes?
- **f** Johnny Depp
- **7** What did most British people have for breakfast this morning?
- **g** Snakes
- **8** Who calls their city *The Big Apple*?
- **h** Insects
- **9** Which city has more Indian restaurants than Mumbai and New Delhi?
- **i** France
- **10** Who played the part of Willy Wonka in the film *Charlie and the Chocolate Factory*?
- **j** W K Kellogg, in 1894

4 Practice

Match answers a–h with 1–8. Then make the questions.

1h What happened in September 1939?

a The number 39.
b The English Channel.
c The Americans.
d They had bread, olives and cheese.
e The Mongolians, in 1299.
f Real Madrid, 5 – 1.
g It means 'very big'.
h The Second World War began.

1 What / happen / in September 1939?
2 Which bus / you usually catch / to school?
3 Who / win / the match last night?
4 What / the Romans / eat / for breakfast?
5 Which sea / separate / England from France?
6 What / 'huge' / mean?
7 Who / invent / lemonade?
8 Which nationality / eat / the most chocolate?

5 Listening and speaking
Brainbox

a 🔊 Listen to part of a TV quiz called *Brainbox*. For each question, write the number of the correct topic.

Q1 = B

A sport
B films
C geography
D books
E science and technology

🔊 Listen and check.

b 🔊 Listen to the second series of questions. Do you know the answers?

c 🔊 Now listen to the questions and the answers.

1 How many answers did you get right?
2 How many answers did Rachel get right?

6 Writing and speaking
Quiz questions

Use what you know

Think of more questions for a quiz and ask your friends.

Who won the last World Cup?
What sort of music did Louis Armstrong play?

In Step 3 you
● read a review of a book
● study adjectives ending in *-ed/-ing*
so that you can
● write a review

1 Share your ideas *Fast food*

Can you give some examples of junk food? Are there many fast food restaurants in your country? Do you ever go to them?

> There are lots of fast food restaurants in the cities.

2 Reading

a Read the review of *Fast Food Nation*. Is the book in favour of fast food or against it?

FAST FOOD NATION

WHAT THE ALL-AMERICAN MEAL IS DOING TO THE WORLD

In his best-selling book *Fast Food Nation*, American writer Eric Schlosser says he used to eat a lot of fast food. It was cheap and convenient and he thought it tasted quite good. But he doesn't eat it any more. His book explains why.

Schlosser describes the amazing size of the fast food business. Americans spend over $100 billion a year on fast food. Every day about a quarter of them visit a fast food restaurant. The three largest companies have more than 60,000 restaurants across the world, and they open several new ones every day.

Schlosser's description of these huge restaurant chains is depressing. The food is prepared in factories, and chemicals are added to improve its taste and smell. From Melbourne to Moscow, the restaurants always look the same. They all serve the same meals, which are cooked by machines. The people who work in the kitchens don't learn any skills and they are very badly paid. Two-thirds of America's fast food workers are under 20.

Young people are also important customers. Advertisements are often designed specially for children, who may get toys and games when they go for a meal. Companies even pay schools to advertise burgers and soft drinks. But these products are unhealthy because they contain a lot of fat and sugar. About 25% of the young people in America are overweight and the problem is getting worse.

I was shocked by the information Schlosser gives us, and I'll certainly think twice before I order my next burger and fries.

b Comprehension check

[cassette icon] Listen, and read the text again. Then answer the questions.

1 Who wrote *Fast Food Nation*?
2 What did he use to enjoy doing in the past?
3 How much do Americans spend on fast food?
4 Do the big fast food companies have restaurants in other countries too?
5 Do the people who work in them earn much money?
6 What helps fast food to taste better?
7 Why do fast food companies sometimes give money to schools?
8 Why are burgers and soft drinks unhealthy?

c Reading skills *Recognising facts and opinions*

Do these sentences give facts or opinions? Write F (fact) or O (opinion).

1 Fast food tastes good.
2 Americans spend over $100 billion a year on fast food.
3 The biggest companies open new restaurants every day.
4 Schlosser's description is depressing.
5 The meals are cooked by machines.

d What do you think? Are there any facts in the text that you found surprising? What are your opinions about the fast food business?

3 Word work
Adjectives ending in -ed/-ing

a Look at the examples, then complete the two lists.

Schlosser's description is **depressing**.
I felt **depressed** when I read his book.

I felt ...	The book was ...
interested	1 *interesting*
2	exciting
bored	3 ....
4	depressing
shocked	5 ....
fascinated	6 ....
7	annoying
amazed	8 ....

b Write adjectives with *-ed* or *-ing*.

1 depressing

1 I don't like stories with sad endings. They're depress...... .
2 Jane's annoy...... because I forgot to ring her last night.
3 I thought the programme was fascinat...... . I'm amaz...... that you didn't like it.
4 I'm not interest...... in golf. I think it's a bor...... game.
5 I think the book is well-written, but it isn't very excit...... .
6 There are rats in that restaurant! It's shock...... !

Writing guide *Writing a review*

● **Paragraph 1**
Give some facts.

The ... Café is in ...
It's open ... days a week, from ... o'clock to ... o'clock.
It serves ... food.

● **Paragraph 2**
Give your opinions.

It's a comfortable, friendly place.
I (don't) like going there because ...
The food is ...

4 Writing *A review*

Use what you know

Write a review for a school magazine about one of these places.

a café   a restaurant   a school canteen
a take-away food shop

The review can be about a place that you know, or about an imaginary place.

Give some facts and then express your opinions.

Extra exercises

1 Read the text. Put the letters in order and make words describing food.

Dad took me to the Boat House restaurant yesterday. For a starter, I ordered ¹*spranw*, and they were very nice, fresh from the sea. For my main course I had ²*neckich* with mushrooms. It was served with ³*eric*, and there was a choice of green vegetables – ⁴*senab*, ⁵*apse* or ⁶*crocobil*. There was also a green salad, but I didn't want that – I'm not keen on ⁷*tucteel*. Finally, I had ⁸*wrestribares* for dessert. It was a very nice meal.

2 Complete the dialogue. Use *some, any* or *no*.

A: Have we got ¹............ apples?

B: No, not at the moment. I bought ²............ bread and ³............ eggs on the way home, but I didn't get ⁴............ fruit. I forgot.

A: But you promised to make an apple tart for dessert.

B: Well, I'm afraid I can't. I've just told you, there are ⁵............ apples. There's ⁶............ fruit in the house at all. You can have ⁷............ ice cream if you like.

A: No, there isn't ⁸............ ice cream. I ate it all last night.

B: Well, that means there's ⁹............ dessert for you tonight, then.

3 Choose the right words.

1 I used to live in the city, but I prefer living in a small town. It's safer here. There's (*a lot of / less*) crime.

2 You look terrible! You need to get (*more / less*) sleep.

3 It would be a fantastic job! I'd work (*less / fewer*) hours and earn (*more / less*) money.

4 Trains are better for the environment than planes because they use (*less / more*) fuel.

5 We should all buy (*fewer / less*) things from abroad and eat (*more / less*) local food.

6 There are (*a lot of / more*) local markets in France than in England.

4 Complete the dialogues. Use *prefer* or *rather* and the words in the box.

be by the window   get a blue one
see the one about food miles   to have prawns
to go to Yellowstone Park

1 A: I like the white one.
  B: I don't. I'd *rather get a blue one.*

2 A: Would you like to sit in the middle?
  B: I'd .... We're going to fly over the Alps!

3 A: The broccoli and cheese soup sounds nice.
  B: I think I'd ....

4 A: Shall we watch the quiz programme?
  B: I'd .... It sounds really interesting.

5 A: Would you like to go to Benidorm?
  B: I'd .... We went to Benidorm last year.

5 Match 1–6 with a–f and make questions.

1	Which team do you	a	last night?
2	What did you	b	write to?
3	Who did you	c	won the match?
4	Who wrote	d	support?
5	What happened	e	do last night?
6	Which team	f	this book?

6 Complete the conversation. Use your imagination.

A: Which cinema did you go to?
B: ¹........................
A: Who else went?
B: ²........................
A: What did you see?
B: ³........................
A: What happened at the end?
B: ⁴........................
A: What did you think of it?
B: ⁵........................

7 How do you say these sentences in your language?

1 It's 5,000 kilometres away.
2 It doesn't make any sense.
3 There are no free seats.
4 We'd prefer to eat fresh food.
5 I'd rather play cards.
6 We import more and more clothes.

Extra reading

Make Poverty History

Have you ever heard of the campaign *Make Poverty History*? What does its title mean?

One day, over twenty years ago, when your parents were listening to their favourite bands, the world of pop music changed for ever. Bob Geldof, the lead singer in a band called The Boomtown Rats, was watching a TV film about the famine in Ethiopia. He was so shocked by what he saw that he decided to do something to help.

He brought together a group of famous singers and musicians and they recorded a song called *Do they know it's Christmas?* (sometimes known as *Feed the World*). This was followed by two concerts – called *Live Aid* – by the world's biggest stars, in London and in Philadelphia, USA. The record and the concerts raised millions of pounds. But poverty didn't go away and people continued to starve.

In the summer of 2005, some of the original stars – and a lot of new ones too – came together at concerts all round the world. This time the concerts were called *Live 8* because they took place at the same time as the G8 meeting – a meeting of eight world leaders in Scotland. The concerts marked the beginning of a new campaign: *Make Poverty History*.

Before the concert in Britain, a quarter of a million people marched through the streets of Edinburgh. Bob Geldof called it the start of 'the long walk to justice' for the world's poorest people. The campaign is a powerful one because it is supported by many rich and famous people. But it will only succeed if everyone works together to achieve a fairer world.

ABOUT POVERTY

- Every day, 30,000 children die as a result of extreme poverty.
- More than 850 million people have not got enough to eat.
- 20% of the world's population own 86% of the world's wealth.
- The three richest people in the world have got more money than all the 600 million people who live in the world's poorest countries.

Task

Read the text, then answer these questions.

1. How long ago did the first *Live Aid* concert take place?
2. Who started the idea of *Live Aid*?
3. Who did he want to help?
4. Did the campaign raise much money?
5. What were the 2005 concerts called?
6. What else was happening in Scotland at that time?
7. What was the new campaign called?
8. Has the campaign had a lot of support?

Grammar check

1 Verb/preposition + -ing form

Work it out for yourself

A Look at the picture, read the sentence and then complete the explanation.

Sara **enjoys** sing**ing** in the choir.

When the verbs *enjoy, can't stand, don't/doesn't mind* are followed by another verb, we use the _____ form of the second verb, and we usually do the same after *like, love, hate, prefer*.

Now make a sentence about Mike.

B Look at the sentences and answer the questions.

She's good **at** draw**ing**.

He's interested **in** cook**ing**.

She isn't keen **on** sail**ing**.

1 Which words in the sentences are prepositions?
2 Which form of the verb do we use after the prepositions?

Check that you can

● use the -*ing* form after verbs and prepositions.

Make sentences using the words in brackets.

1 I like going to football matches.

1 I go to a lot of football matches. (*like/go*)
2 Jenny's scared when she's in a crowd. (*can't stand/be*)
3 Ben's always ill when he travels by car. (*hate/travel*)
4 I don't want to be in the choir. (*not good at/sing*)
5 Jay always takes his surfboard when he goes to the beach. (*keen on/surf*)
6 Jack often tidies his room. It isn't a problem. (*doesn't mind/tidy*)

2 *want/ask/tell* someone to do something

Work it out for yourself

1 *She wants **Ben to wear** a helmet.*

2 SUE: *He's asked **me to go** to the cinema!*

3 *He told **her to go** to bed.*

Match the words in sentences 2 and 3 with the pattern in the table.

subject	*want/ask/tell*	noun/object pronoun	*to*	verb
She	wants	Ben	to	wear

Check that you can

● use the right pattern after *want/ask/tell*.

Complete the sentences about a school trip.

1 The teacher wants Helen to come on the trip.

1 'Helen, I hope you'll come on the trip.' The teacher wants Helen ...
2 'Listen, everyone. Bring a packed lunch.' She wants them ...
3 'The coach leaves at nine. You mustn't be late.' She doesn't want ...
4 'You must wear warm clothes.' She told ...
5 'Paul, bring your video camera.' She told ...
6 'Jenny, can you phone Helen this evening?' She asked ...

3 Expressions of quantity
Work it out for yourself

A Match the sentences with pictures A and B.

1 There's **more** broccoli in this shop.
2 There isn't **any** cheese.
3 There are **more** beans in this shop.
4 There are **no** prawns.
5 There aren't **any** prawns.
6 There are **fewer** beans in this shop.
7 There's **less** broccoli in this shop.
8 There's **no** cheese.

B Answer the questions.

1 In the list in A, which sentences mean the same?
   Sentence 2 = sentence ....
   Sentence .... = sentence ....

2 *Fewer* and *less* mean the same, but which do we use with countable nouns, and which with uncountable nouns?

Check that you can

● use expressions of quantity.

Choose the right answer.

1 There aren't (*some / any*) shops near our house.
2 We've got some rice, but there are (*some / no*) vegetables.
3 I've got (*less / fewer*) patience than you.
4 We need (*more / fewer*) singers if we want a choir.
5 I can't give you (*no / any*) money.
6 (*Fewer / Less*) people write letters now.

4 Subject and object questions
Work it out for yourself

A Look at the picture and match questions 1 and 2 with answers a and b.

1 *What **hit** the car?*
2 *What **did** the car **hit**?*

a It hit the woman's bike.
b The bus hit it.

B Complete the explanations with *object* and *subject*.

When we ask about the .... , we use *do/does/did*. When we ask about the .... , we **don't** use *do/does/did*.

Check that you can

● use the right verb form after *What/ Who/Which*.

Write the questions for these answers.

1 What does 'brainy' mean?

1 It means 'very clever'. (What / 'brainy' / mean ?)
2 The English. (Who / invent / the game of rugby ?)
3 The computer. (What / Charles Babbage / invent ?)
4 Toast and coffee. (What / you / have / for breakfast ?)
5 Our team won. (Which team / win / the final ?)
6 Paul and Helen. (Who / you / see / in town ?)
7 The red one. (Which T-shirt / you / like ?)
8 A ball, I think. (What / break / the window ?)

Vocabulary and expressions

People in groups
audience
band
choir
club
crowd
gang
orchestra
team

Likes and dislikes
(to) dislike
(to) enjoy
(to) hate
(to) like
I can't stand …
I don't mind …
I'm good at …
I'm keen on …
I'm useless at …

Requests and responses
Can you lend me …?
Could you tell me …?
Would you mind opening …?
Would you take …?

Yes, of course.
I guess so, but …
No, of course not. No problem.
I'm afraid I can't. Sorry, but …

A wildlife commentary
ant
beside
brave
crocodile
(to) defend
fox
in return
jaws
nest
parasite
plover
protection
relationship
sharp

social system
species

Food
beans
broccoli
carrots
cheese
chicken
lettuce
peas
prawns
rice
strawberries

Expressing preferences
I'd rather walk …
We'd prefer to eat …

The fast food industry
best-selling
chain
chemicals
convenient
fat (n.)
in favour of
junk food
overweight
(to) prepare
product
smell (n.)
soft drink
specially
take-away food
taste (n.)
(to) taste (good)
toy

Adjectives ending in -ed/-ing
amazed / amazing
annoyed / annoying
bored / boring
depressed / depressing
excited / exciting
fascinated / fascinating
interested / interesting
shocked / shocking

Study skills 5
Preparing and giving a talk

Giving a short talk to the class is a very good way to practise your English. Here are some suggestions for giving a talk.

1 Choose a topic which really interests you, and which is familiar to you.
2 Write your ideas in rough first.
3 Find information in books and on the Internet.
4 Think of a way to introduce your topic (*I'd like to talk about … because …*), and a way to finish your talk (*I hope you enjoyed learning more about …*). You might like to say why the topic interests you.
5 Make notes on a card. Write key words – don't write full sentences.
6 Speak to the class directly – don't read a prepared text.
7 You could practise your talk at home, and record it.
8 Your talk doesn't have to be very long. Two minutes is plenty.

When you have studied Unit 10 Step 1, you might like to prepare and give a short talk to the class. You can use Clare's talk (page 102) as a model.

How's it going?

- ### Your rating

Look again at pages 110 and 111. For each section decide on your rating: Good ✓ ✓ ✓   Not bad ✓ ✓
I can't remember much ✓

- ### Vocabulary

Choose three words from the list and read them to a friend. Your friend writes them down, then makes a sentence with each word. Check your friend's sentences.

- ### Test a friend

Look again at Units 9 and 10. Think of at least two questions, then ask a friend.

Who went on a school trip?   Why is fast food bad for you?

- ### Correcting mistakes

Can you correct these mistakes? In some sentences, there is more than one mistake.

1 ~~Which pop group did sing Hey Jude?~~
2 ~~I don't mind to meet new people and I love go to parties.~~
3 ~~Charlotte asked that I have dinner with her.~~
4 ~~There are fewer pollution in the country than in the city.~~
5 ~~Do you like come to my house next weekend?~~

- ### Your Workbook

Complete the Learning Diaries for Units 9 and 10.

Coursework 5 — Our school magazine

Read the adverts in this month's edition of *Pulse*. Then make at least two similar adverts about things in your community.

The ads page

GREENSIDE COMMUNITY TENNIS

Whitley Gardens, Shaw Street.

We have classes for
- all ages
- all abilities
- all seasons

Telephone Paul: 07991 776654
or Tanya: 06754 987675

BISTRO 7
restaurant and café

Open Tuesday to Sunday
for lunch and dinner.

7 Lime Street
(Opposite St George's Hall)
0151 978624

CALLING ALL GLASTONBURY FANS!

I've got 2 tickets for sale for the Glastonbury Festival. £50 each.

Rob Snelson Class 4N

CHESS CLUB

Thursday 4.30 pm
Room 103

If you're good at solving problems and you like a challenge, then you'll love playing chess.

Why don't you try it?

Who wants to be our next Pavarotti?

Do you enjoy singing?
Come and join us!
We need more people for the school choir.

We meet every Wednesday afternoon at 4.00 pm

Contact: Wendy Newman Room 32

BIKE FOR SALE

Mountain bike for sale

2005 in excellent condition

Also helmet (size: medium)

£119

Contact Nat Harris Room 84
nharris@greensidecc.net

MATHS TUITION

Are you worried about your maths?

Call me for expert, friendly help.

I offer private lessons in the evening or at the weekend.

JENNY GARDNER
0151 321564

Module 6

Just imagine!

In Module 6 Steps 1 and 2 you study

Grammar
- Past perfect
- *must, can't, might, could* for speculation
- Reported speech
- *say* and *tell*

Vocabulary
- Adjectives describing feelings
- Words connected with money

Expressions
- *Neither do I. So am I.*
- Everyday expressions

so that you can
- Talk about feelings
- Show that one past action happened before another past action
- Talk about what you imagine is true
- Show agreement and similarity
- Talk about money
- Report what people say
- Make a conversation at a party

In Step 3 you ...

read
- A story about an extraordinary experience
- Three jumbled stories

study
- Adverbs
- Phrasal verbs
- Guessing meaning from context
- Following the sequence of a story

so that you can
- Write a short story
- Write and reply to a message

Life and culture

Gandhi
Keeping in touch

What's it about?

What can you say about the pictures?

Now match the pictures with sentences 1–5.

1 They managed to climb to the top successfully.
2 They said that money wasn't the key to happiness.
3 ... the wind in the sails, the open sea! It must be great.
4 She put a message in a bottle and threw it into the sea.
5 The storm had completely destroyed our house.

11 Challenges

In Step 1 you study
- adjectives describing feelings
- past perfect

so that you can
- talk about feelings
- describe events and feelings in the past

1 Key vocabulary *Feelings*

a 🕐 📻 Listen to the adjectives, then work with a friend. How do you say them in your language? You've got three minutes!

> annoyed   disappointed   embarrassed
> fed up   lonely   nervous   pleased
> relaxed   relieved   surprised   upset
> worried

b **What about you?** How would you feel in these situations? Choose at least one adjective each time.

1   You arrive at school and your teacher says, 'We aren't going to have any lessons today. We're going to have a party.'
2   You've got an important exam later today.
3   You lost your wallet yesterday. A friend has just rung and said, 'Don't worry! I've found it.'
4   It's Saturday night. All your friends have gone to the cinema, but you're at home on your own.
5   You worked hard before a test but your marks weren't very good.
6   You've just been to the hairdresser's but your hair looks awful.

c Think of more adjectives describing feelings. *angry, ...*

2 Presentation *Our house had disappeared*

a What can you say about the photos?

b 📻 Close your book and listen to Shelley's story. Were she and her family injured in the tornado?

Shelley Wood will never forget the day when her house in Florida was destroyed by a tornado. This is her story.

SHELLEY: It was an evening in May. I'd spent the day at home with my brother and my mum. The weather had been warm and dry – nothing unusual. But, when I went to bed, I could hear the rain and wind outside. I felt quite worried because there had been tornadoes nearby in the past, but we'd never had one in my town. My dad was away on business. He'd always told us to hide in the cupboard in the hall if there was a tornado.

In the middle of the night I woke up. My mum was screaming, 'Shelley! Get in the cupboard!' Everything was black. I followed my mum and we all lay on the floor of the cupboard. There was an incredible noise. Then, a few moments later, it was over. We stood up and looked around. The storm had completely destroyed our house.

We walked to a neighbour's house and then, in the morning, we went back. My room and all my possessions had disappeared. I found some jeans in the garden. That was all. We have a new house now, with a storm shelter. But I still feel nervous when I hear the wind.

c Listen again and follow in your book. Then put these events in the right order (1–8).

a The storm destroyed their house.

b Shelley went to bed.

c Shelley's dad told them to hide in the cupboard.

d Shelley and her mum and brother spent the night at a neighbour's house.

e Her dad went away on business.

f Shelley found her jeans in the garden.

g Her mum told her to get in the cupboard.

h They went back to their house.

 Listen and check.

3 Key grammar *Past perfect*

Look at the examples and read the explanation. Which action on the time line happened first?

```
←-------------------------------- PAST        NOW
         |                    |
The storm had         We went back
destroyed our house.  to our house.
```

We use the past perfect to show that one action in the past happened before another action in the past.

We form the past perfect using had ('d) + *past participle:* had destroyed. *Note how we form negatives and questions:* There **hadn't been** a tornado in their town before. What **had** Shelley's dad **told** his family?

G ➤ 10a-b

4 Practice

a Put the words in the right order and make sentences in the past perfect.

1 dad / gone / where / Shelley's / had ?

2 tornado / hundreds / destroyed / of / the / trees / had

3 hadn't / Shelley / that / friends / seen / her / day

4 spent / the / Shelley / day / had / home / at ?

5 happened / their / what / house / had / to ?

b Complete the sentences with verbs in the past perfect.

1 Nadia was angry because someone *had broken* (*break*) her CD case.

2 The classroom was empty. Everyone .... (*go*) home.

3 Alice was upset because Tom .... (*not tell*) her the truth.

4 After I .... (*do*) the washing up, I did my homework.

5 Luke couldn't find his camera. He .... (*left*) it on the coach.

6 Mrs Gray was worried because Danny .... (*not contact*) her.

7 We were relieved because no one .... (*see*) us.

Try this!
Match the two halves of each word and make six past participles.
GO BRO SE DISAP LE SP
KEN OKEN NE FT PEARED EN

5 Listening and speaking
A terrible night

a Listen to the man's story. Who do you think he is?

b Listen again. How did the man feel at these times during the story? Why did he feel like that?

1 before he turned on the TV

2 after he had seen the news on TV

3 after he had received the phone call

6 Writing *What had happened?*

Use what you know

Choose one of the feelings from Exercise 1 and write a short description of a situation in the past. How did you feel? Why? What had happened?

I was really surprised when I got home yesterday. My brother had cleaned our flat and he'd cooked the dinner.

In Step 2 you study
- *must, can't, might, could* for speculation
- *Neither do I. So am I.*

so that you can
- talk about what you imagine is true
- show agreement and similarity

1 Share your ideas

Look at the ship in the photo. Would you like to sail on one? What do you think it would be like?

> I'd like to go on a ship like that.

2 Presentation *It must be great*

a 🔊 Listen to the conversation and follow in your book. Which of the four friends would like to go on one of the ships?

The Mersey River Festival takes place in Liverpool every June. Danny and his friends are there now. They're sitting by the water, looking at the old sailing ships.

DANNY: I love those old sailing ships.

NADIA: Yes, so do I. They're beautiful.

DANNY: I think there are special trips for young people. They teach you how to sail the ship. I wonder what it's like.

CLARE: I think it could be fun, but it might be expensive.

LUKE: Fun? I don't think so. It must be really hard work.

NADIA: I wouldn't mind that. Imagine – the wind in the sails, the open sea. Oh, it must be great.

CLARE: It can't be very nice when the weather's bad. I bet everyone's seasick.

DANNY: Look at those guys at the top of the mast! I don't fancy that.

CLARE: No, neither do I.

NADIA: But what a fantastic experience! A real challenge! I'd love to try it.

LUKE: What's the time? I'm getting hungry.

DANNY: So am I. Hey, Nadia, if you want a challenge, how about getting us some sandwiches from that stall? The end of the queue must be round the corner somewhere!

b Read the conversation again. Then read these sentences. How many false sentences can you find?

1 Nadia agrees with Danny. She likes the ships too.

2 Clare doesn't know how much the special trips cost.

3 Luke thinks that a trip on a sailing ship would be fun.

4 Nadia thinks she'd enjoy it.

5 Clare wouldn't want to be at sea in bad weather.

6 Danny and Clare wouldn't like to climb to the top of the mast.

7 Luke and Danny are both hungry.

3 Key grammar
must, can't, might, could *for speculation*

Look at the examples and the explanation. How do you say these sentences in your language?

> I'd love to try it. It **must** be great.
> The sailing trips **might/could** be expensive.
> It **can't** be very nice when the weather's bad.
>
> *We use* must + *verb when we think that something is true.*
> *We use* might *or* could + *verb when we think that something is possible.*
> *We use* can't + *verb when we think that something is impossible.*

G ▸ 18

4 Practice

a Complete the sentences with *must* or *can't*.

1 I'm sorry you didn't pass your driving test. You .... be really disappointed.
2 You .... be hungry! You've just had your lunch.
3 I don't believe you. It's a lie. It .... be true!
4 They .... have lots of money. They've got a boat and a helicopter.
5 He wants to sail across the Atlantic in a bath! He .... be crazy!
6 She .... be eighteen. She's the same age as my brother and he's sixteen.
7 It .... be 30th February, because there aren't 30 days in February.
8 The Grays have lived in Liverpool for a long time. They .... know lots of people there.

b Look at the five parcels. What do you think they are? Write your ideas, then share them with the class. Use *might* or *could*.

It might/could be an umbrella.

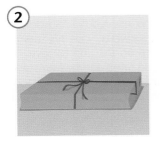

5 Key expressions So/Neither ... I.

A: I love those ships.
B: Yes, so do I.

A: I don't fancy that.
B: No, neither do I.

A: I'm not sure.
B: Neither am I.

A: I've got some sandwiches.
B: So have I.

Work with a friend and make six dialogues. One person reads a sentence and the other agrees.

1 I hate exams.
2 I'm hungry.
3 I haven't got enough money.
4 I don't fancy fish for lunch.
5 I've got a rucksack.
6 I'm not going out tonight.

6 Key pronunciation
Stress in sentences; weak forms

Listen and repeat the sentences. Practise the weak forms and the links between the words.

1 Neither am I.
2 So are you.
3 Neither does he.
4 So do I.
5 Neither has she.
6 So have they.

7 Speaking *What's it like?*

Use what you know

Choose at least two of these situations and imagine what they are like.

– singing in front of a huge audience
– travelling in a submarine
– walking on the moon
– standing on the top of Mount Everest

Work with a friend and make sentences.

It might be uncomfortable.

It must be fantastic!

STEP 3

In Step 3 you
● read a story
● study adverbs
so that you can
● write a short story

1 Share your ideas
In the mountains

a Look at the photos and think of words associated with mountains.

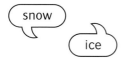

snow

ice

b What problems and dangers could there be for people in this environment?

It must be very cold at night.

2 Reading

a Read the text about Joe Simpson and Simon Yates. What is the story about? Choose the best answer.

   a bad weather in the Andes

   b mountain climbing

   c an extraordinary experience

On the edge

Joe Simpson and Simon Yates were the first people to climb the West Face of the Siula Grande in the Andes mountains. They reached the top successfully but on their way back conditions were very difficult. Joe fell and broke his leg.

They both knew that if Simon continued alone, he would probably get back safely. But Simon decided to risk his life and try to lower Joe down the mountain on a rope. The weather got worse as they went down. Then another disaster happened. They couldn't see or hear each other and, by mistake, Simon lowered his friend over the edge of a precipice.

It was impossible for Joe to climb back and impossible for Simon to pull him up. Joe's weight was pulling Simon slowly towards the precipice. Finally, after more than an hour in the dark and the icy cold, Simon had to make a decision. He cut the rope.

Joe fell into a huge crevasse in the ice below – but he survived. He had no food or water and he was in terrible pain. He couldn't walk, but he managed to get out of the crevasse. Then he started to hop and crawl towards their camp, nearly ten kilometres away.

Simon had returned to the camp at the foot of the mountain. He thought that Joe must be dead, but he didn't want to leave immediately. Three days later, in the middle of the night, he heard Joe's voice calling his name. He couldn't believe it. Joe was there, a few metres from their tent, still alive.

Simon felt guilty about cutting the rope, but both men believed he had done everything possible to save his friend. 'He put his life on the line to save mine,' Joe said later. Joe has written a book called *Touching the Void* about their extraordinary experiences, and it is now also a film.

b Reading skills

Guessing meaning from context

Find these words in the text. Try to guess what they mean. Share your ideas.

reached   safely   lower   precipice   crevasse
managed   hop   crawl

c Comprehension check

[cassette icon] **Listen, and read the text again. These sentences are all false. Can you give the correct information?**

1 Joe broke his leg on the way back.

1 Joe had broken his leg before he reached the top of the mountain.
2 Simon decided to help Joe because he knew they would get back safely.
3 Simon could see that Joe was near the edge of a precipice.
4 Joe managed to climb back.
5 Simon cut the rope because he was very cold.
6 After he had fallen, Joe walked for several days.
7 When Joe reached their camp, Simon had gone.
8 Later, Joe felt angry with Simon.

3 Word work *Adverbs*

Look at the examples.

They reached the top **successfully**.
He was moving **slowly** towards the precipice.

Adverbs tell us more about a verb.

We form most adverbs by adding *-ly* to the adjective:

successful > **successfully**   slow > **slowly**

But not all adverbs follow this rule:

early > **early**   fast > **fast**   good > **well**
hard > **hard**   late > **late**

Read the sentences and choose the right words.

1 I was (*sad / sadly*) when we had to say goodbye.
2 The man ran (*quick / quickly*) round the corner.
3 We could hear (*loud / loudly*) voices in the flat next door.
4 It was a difficult journey but we all arrived (*safe / safely*).
5 I get (*nervous / nervously*) when I'm in a big crowd.
6 'Stop that!' she shouted (*angry / angrily*).
7 We haven't been to London (*recent / recently*).
8 I can't sing very (*good / well*).

Writing guide *Writing a story*

● **Paragraph 1**
Set the scene. Introduce the place and the character(s).

It was a sunny afternoon / a cold night in …
Liz and Bill were …

● **Paragraph 2**
Describe how the dangerous situation developed.

Suddenly, …
They tried to … , but …

● **Paragraph 3**
Describe how the characters escaped from the situation.
Then/After that …
They managed to …
Finally, …

4 Writing *A short story*

Use what you know

Think of a situation where someone was in danger, for example:

– a storm or a fire
– a problem on a mountain or at sea
– a meeting with a wild animal
– your own ideas

Write a short story.

Who was/were the character(s)? Where were they?
How did the situation develop? How did the characters feel?
How did they manage to escape from danger?

Read your story to a friend.

Extra exercises

1 Match 1–6 with a–f and make six sentences.

1 I couldn't play football because
2 When I went back to the shop
3 Helen was upset yesterday because
4 We got to the theatre after
5 I didn't wait for you because
6 When I arrived at the airport

a I hadn't read your text message.
b the plane had just landed.
c I hadn't brought my boots.
d the play had started.
e they'd sold all the cheap trainers.
f I hadn't remembered her birthday.

2 Write sentences using the words in brackets. Use the past perfect form of the verbs.

1 When Erica arrived, Tom wasn't at home. (*He / go / to the leisure centre*)
2 We had to leave the car and walk into town. (*We / run out of petrol*)
3 I couldn't find the way to Lynn's house. (*She / not give / me any directions*)
4 I was relieved when I found my wallet. (*I / leave / it in the post office*)
5 Scientists were surprised that the volcano was active. (*It / not erupt / for 250 years*)
6 When Liz came out of the shop, her bike wasn't there. (*Someone / steal / it*)

3 Choose the right adjective.

1 When I forgot the words of the song, everyone laughed. I was so _____ !
   a worried   b disappointed   c embarrassed

2 Our teachers get _____ if we make a lot of noise in class.
   a annoyed   b lonely   c surprised

3 When the tornado hit the city, my aunt was staying there. We were _____ when we heard that she was OK.
   a upset   b relieved   c relaxed

4 A lot of people feel _____ when they go in a plane.
   a fed up   b nervous   c lonely

5 No one was _____ when Diane got the best results in art. Her paintings are brilliant.
   a surprised   b pleased   c worried

6 Harry really wanted to play in the basketball team, but he wasn't chosen. He was very _____ .
   a disappointed   b relaxed   c pleased

4 Complete the sentences. Use *must, can't, might* or *could.*

1 I don't know where Danny is. He _____ be at Luke's place.
2 That bike _____ be Clare's. She hasn't got one.
3 It's only got six legs, so it _____ be a spider.
4 Paul's won the poetry competition. He _____ be pleased.
5 These earrings _____ be made of gold, but I'm not sure.
6 You didn't get much sleep last night. You _____ be tired.

5 Complete the conversation. Choose from a–h.

A: Let's have some lunch. I'm hungry.
B: ¹ _____
A: I'm not sure. I haven't got much money.
B: ² _____
A: OK, but I don't want a sandwich.
B: ³ _____
A: There's some chicken curry in the fridge, but I'm not very keen on curry.
B: ⁴ _____
A: I know. I'll make some soup. I love soup.
B: ⁵ _____

a No, neither do I.
b Yes, so have I.
c So am I. Shall we go to the café?
d So do I. What are you going to put in it?
e So am I. I love curry.
f Neither am I. I didn't have any breakfast.
g No, neither have I. Let's make something.
h Neither am I. And we had it for dinner last night.

6 How do you say these sentences in your language?

1 I wonder what it's like.
2 I don't fancy that.
3 It could be fun.
4 He managed to climb up the rope.
5 What a fantastic experience!
6 A: I don't like that guy.
   B: Neither do I.

Extra reading

Life and culture

Gandhi

Who do you think teenage boys in Britain see as their hero?
Who do teenage boys in your country admire?

According to a recent survey, the person that most teenage boys in Britain admire is Mahatma Gandhi.

Gandhi was born in India in 1869. At that time, the country was ruled by the British.

He was educated in India and in Britain and he worked as a lawyer. He got married when he was 13 and he and his wife Kasturbai had four children. He lived a simple life with few possessions and his religion, Hinduism, was very important to him. He hated violence and he was a strict vegetarian.

For many years Gandhi worked in South Africa. There were different rules for white South Africans and for Indians and black South Africans. One day a white policeman told Gandhi to get off a train because of the colour of his skin. He was so angry that he decided to fight for the rights of Indians. But he told his supporters that they must not use violence.

Gandhi returned to India in 1915 and he became a leader of the campaign for India's independence – a campaign which lasted for more than thirty years. He and his followers refused to obey British laws, but their protests were always peaceful. They went to prison many times.

His most famous protest was against the 'salt law' – people had to pay the government when they took salt from the beaches. Gandhi and his followers walked 20 kilometres a day, for three weeks, to get to the beach. They took

the salt but they refused to pay anything. Thousands followed their example and many of them went to prison, but the British knew they had lost control of the people of India.

On August 15th 1947, India finally won its independence, but the country was divided into two: India and Pakistan, and Gandhi was deeply disappointed. He was assassinated in 1948. The Indian Prime Minister, Nehru, said: '… the light that shone in this country was no ordinary light. … that light represented the living truth …'.

ABOUT INDIA

Over one billion people live in India and it is the world's largest democracy. Its capital city is New Delhi and its currency is the rupee.

Task

Read the text and these sentences. For each sentence, write T (true), F (false) or ? (the text doesn't say).

1 When Gandhi was born, India was an independent country.
2 Gandhi went to school in London.
3 He had worked for Indian rights before he returned to India.
4 When he went back to India, he encouraged his supporters to attack the British.
5 Gandhi spent a lot of time in prison.
6 He and his followers walked to the beach to buy salt.
7 More than thirty years after Gandhi's return, India won its independence.
8 Gandhi wanted the country to be divided into two.

12 Happy endings

In Step 1 you study	so that you can
● 'money' words	● talk about money
● reported speech (1)	● report what people say

1 Key vocabulary *Money*

a ⏱ Match the words in 1–9 with definitions a–i. You've got three minutes!

1 Could you **lend** me ten dollars?
2 It's too expensive. I can't **afford** it.
3 Don't **spend** too much at the shops!
4 I've just opened a **bank account**.
5 Have you got a **credit card**?
6 I don't like asking for help. I never **borrow** money.
7 I can't buy anything. I'm **broke**, as usual.
8 There's a **cashpoint** over there.
9 Have you got any **change**? I need some money for the car park.

a (*noun*) a plastic card which we use to pay for things

b (*adj.*) (informal) having no money

c (*noun*) a system for keeping your money in a bank

d (*verb*) to use money to buy things

e (*verb*) to have enough money for something

f (*noun*) smaller units of money, usually coins

g (*verb*) to give something to someone, when we expect to get it back

h (*verb*) to get/take something from someone, when we expect to give it back

i (*noun*) a machine, often in the wall outside a bank, where you can get money

🔊 Listen and check.

b **What about you?** Make at least three true sentences about yourself using words from 1a.

I don't like lending people money.

2 Presentation *What did they say?*

a 🔊 Close your book and listen to Beth. Is money the key to happiness?

Beth is presenting a radio programme called 'Money – the key to happiness?'

BETH: Is money the key to happiness? Well, a recent study of 65 different countries found that the richest people certainly weren't the happiest. I wanted to find out why. First, I talked to two people, Kerry and Dennis Hart, who recently won £10 million on the lottery. I asked them about being rich.

They both thought that it had advantages and disadvantages, and that family and friends were much more important. Kerry said she was going to buy a car for everyone in the family and Dennis said he was hoping to buy his local football club. They wanted to get a new house, but they didn't want to move too far from their friends. Kerry said she'd probably retire but Dennis said he wouldn't stop working because he really enjoyed his job. They both said that money wasn't the answer to all their problems, and it certainly wasn't the key to happiness.

Try this!

How many words can you make using the letters in

CASHPOINT

ship, ...

b 📻 Listen again and follow in your book. What did Kerry and Dennis actually say? Complete the sentences.

> It's got advantages and disadvantages.

1 It's got ...
2 Family and friends are ...
3 I'm going to ...
4 I'm hoping to ...
5 We want to ...
6 We don't want ...
7 I'll probably ...
8 I won't ... because I really ...
9 Money isn't ... and it certainly ...

3 Key grammar *Reported speech (1)*

a Complete the examples and read the explanation.

Direct speech	Reported speech
'It's got advantages.'	They thought (that) it had advantages.
'Friends are more important.'	They said (that) friends were more important.
'I'm going to buy a car.'	She said she _____ going to buy a car.
'We want to get a new house.'	They said they _____ to get a new house.
'I'll probably retire.'	She said she'd probably retire. (she'd = she would)
'I won't stop working.'	He said he _____ stop working.

When we report what someone said, we often make these changes:
present tense > past tense
will > would

We sometimes use that *in reported speech, but we often omit it:*
They said (that) friends were more important.

G ➤ 21a

b What happens to pronouns and possessive adjectives in reported speech? Complete the examples.

> '**I**'m going to buy a car for everyone in **my** family,' she said.
> She said _____ was going to buy a car for everyone in _____ family.

G ➤ 21b

4 Practice

Write sentences starting with *He/She/They said ...*

1 *He said that he wanted to buy a parrot.*

1 'I want to buy a parrot,' he said.
2 'I'm going to open a bank account,' she said.
3 'We can't afford a holiday,' they said.
4 'I'll lend Ben my football boots,' he said.
5 'We won't be late,' they said.
6 'There's a cashpoint near our house,' they said.
7 'I don't like borrowing money,' he said.
8 'Luke isn't in my class,' she said.

5 Key pronunciation
Vowel sounds

📻 Close your book. Listen and repeat the words. Find the odd one out each time.

1 rich   reach   quick   ship
2 bank   cash   match   said
3 broke   road   gone   hope

6 Writing and speaking
Your report

Use what you know

Work with a friend. Imagine your friend has just won the lottery. Ask him/her questions, then report your findings.

> Paul said he was going to put all his money in the bank.

In Step 2 you study
- reported speech (2)
- *say* and *tell*
- everyday expressions

so that you can
- make a conversation at a party

1 Share your ideas

Look at the photo. How many of the people do you recognise? What are their names and what can you say about them?

> I can see Winston and Lorina. They live at Mandela Court.

2 Presentation *What did you tell him?*

a 🔊 Listen to the conversation and follow in your book. Why are the Grays having a party?

The Grays are having a party at their flat in Mandela Court.

BETH: Karim, hi. Come in! Welcome!

KARIM: Hi, Beth. Nice to see you.

BETH: Put your jacket in the bedroom. The food and everything's in the kitchen. Help yourself!

KARIM: Thanks, Beth.

WINSTON: Lyn, we're going now, I'm afraid. We have to get up early tomorrow. We're going to Jamaica.

MRS GRAY: Oh! OK. Well, have a good holiday.

LORINA: I'm sure we will. Thanks for inviting us. We've had a great time. Bye.

MRS GRAY: Bye.

MR GRAY: Danny, who was that on the phone?

DANNY: It was Mr Pringle – you know, the man at number seven. He said he and his wife couldn't sleep because the music was too loud.

MR GRAY: Well, I hope you told him you'd turn it down.

DANNY: Yes, I did. But he said he was going to call the police.

MR GRAY: The police! What did you say?

DANNY: I told him we were really disappointed that they hadn't come to the party. I said we'd sent them an invitation.

MR GRAY: But that's not true!

DANNY: I know, but it worked. He was really pleased. He told me they'd go and get ready.

MR GRAY: What? ... That's the doorbell. It must be the Pringles. Oh, no!

DANNY: Dad! It's your birthday. Relax and enjoy yourself. And don't worry, I'll go and turn down the music ...

b Read the conversation again. Then answer these questions.

1 Is there anything to eat at the party?
2 Why are Winston and Lorina leaving the party now?
3 Do Mr and Mrs Pringle live at Mandela Court?
4 Why did Mr Pringle telephone the Grays?
5 What did Mr Pringle say he was going to do?
6 Danny told a lie. What was it?
7 Did Mr Pringle decide to go to the Grays' party?
8 Is Mr Gray pleased?

3 Key grammar
Reported speech (2); say *and* tell

a Look at the examples and the explanation.

> **Direct speech**
> 'We're disappointed you haven't come.'
> 'We sent you an invitation.'
>
> **Reported speech**
> I said we were disappointed they hadn't come.
> I said we'd sent him an invitation. (we'd = we had)
>
> *In reported speech, we often make these changes:*
> present perfect > past perfect
> past simple > past perfect

 21a

b Look at the examples and complete the explanation with *say* and *tell*.

> He **said** they couldn't sleep.
> I **told** him we were really disappointed.
>
> *We use _____ , and not _____ , when we say who we are talking to.*

 22

4 Practice

a Complete the sentences with the correct form of *say* or *tell*.

1 Mr Pringle *told* Danny he was going to call the police.
2 Beth _____ Karim there was some food in the kitchen.
3 Luke _____ he couldn't find his coat.
4 Winston _____ Lorina that he wanted to leave.
5 Lorina _____ she needed to pack their things.
6 Danny _____ that they'd sent an invitation to the Pringles.
7 Mr Pringle _____ Danny that they hadn't received an invitation.
8 Danny _____ Mr Pringle that he'd get him a drink.

b Now write what the people in 4a actually said.

1 *'I'm going to call the police.'*

5 Key expressions *Everyday expressions*

Nice to see you.   Help yourself.
Have a good holiday.   We had a great time.
Enjoy yourself.

Match the expressions with these sentences. Then work with a friend and make five dialogues.

> Did you enjoy the party?

> Yes, we had a great time.

1 Did you enjoy the party?
2 I'm going to a concert tonight.
3 Can I have some more bread?
4 We're going to Scotland tomorrow.
5 Hi! Come in!

6 Listening *Song*

a 🔊 Listen to the song. How do you think the singer feels?

b 🔊 Copy the words below, then listen again. Tick the words when you hear them. Which word isn't in the song?

clouds   rain   bright   wind
rainbow   'sunshiny'   blue skies

7 Speaking *Party*

Use what you know

Imagine you're having a party. A neighbour phones to say you're making too much noise. Make a conversation with a friend at the party. Use sentences from Exercise 2.

In Step 3 you
● read three short stories
● study phrasal verbs

so that you can
● write and reply to a message

1 Share your ideas
Sending messages

How do you send messages to your friends and family? How did people use to send messages before we had telephones and computers?

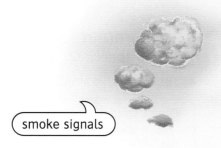

smoke signals

2 Reading

a Read the opening paragraphs from three different stories. The stories have got one thing in common. What do you think it is?

Messages

1

a Eleven-year-old Joanna Tate from Edinburgh had always liked stories about pirates. 'That's how I knew about messages in bottles,' she says.

2

b Miguel de Santo and his brother were fishing 12 kilometres from the coast of Costa Rica when their boat hit some rocks on a tiny island and started to sink.

3

c In the 1920s, scientists often used messages in bottles to help them find out about the currents in the ocean.

b Reading skills *Following the sequence of a story*
Read these sentences and complete the three stories.
Story 1: a, f, i, ...

d People were asked to reply to the message, saying when and where they had found the bottle, and they were promised a small payment in return.

e Before they left the boat and climbed over the rocks to the island, they wrote a message and put it in a bottle.

f One day, when she was travelling on the ferry to France on holiday, she put a message in a bottle and threw it into the English Channel.

◆

g It said 'Help! We're on Esperanza Island.'

h Robert Sellers was playing on the beach near his home in Wales when he found one of the bottles.

i It was found on a beach in Holland by Willem Roemer, who was also eleven years old.

◆

j He wrote to the address in Edinburgh, and after that the two children started to write to each other regularly.

k Six days later, two children picked up a bottle floating in the water near the Colombian town of Cartagena.

l He took it home and read the message. He immediately replied with details of the date and place.

◆

m They took out the message and showed it to their parents, who immediately contacted the police.

n During the next ten years they met several times, and finally they fell in love.

o Three weeks later, some money and a letter of thanks arrived in the post.

◆

p After almost a week without food, the two brothers had nearly given up hope. Then they saw the rescue boat. The message in the bottle had saved them.

q After that, he often went to the beach, but he didn't find any more messages. But, when he grew up, he became a marine scientist himself.

r Now they've been happily married for over 25 years, and they've still got the bottle and the message that brought them together.

🔊 Listen to the complete stories.

c Comprehension check

Look at the three stories again. Then answer these questions.

1 Who fell in love as a result of a message in a bottle?
2 Whose lives were saved by their message?
3 Who chose a job which was connected to his message?
4 Where was Joanna Tate when she wrote her message?
5 Who found the message from Miguel and his brother?
6 Why did Robert want to find more messages, do you think?

Remember!

Whose lives were saved? – Miguel and his brother's.
Whose jacket is this? / **Whose** is this jacket? – It's mine.
Whose = Who does it belong to?

3 Word work *Phrasal verbs*

Look at the examples.

Two children **picked up** a bottle.
They wanted to **find out** about ocean currents.

Complete the sentences with the verbs in the box.

find out	give up	grow up	pick up	put on
take off	take out	turn down	turn off	turn on

1 I want to watch the news. Would you _____ the TV?
2 _____ your boots when you go out. It's snowing outside.
3 Please _____ your computer if you aren't using it.
4 Don't _____ ! I'm sure you'll succeed if you try again.
5 People always _____ their shoes before they go into a mosque.
6 Children become more independent as they _____ .
7 I don't know the answer, but I'll try to _____ for you.
8 Can you _____ your clothes? They're all over the floor.
9 Would you _____ the music? It's incredibly loud!
10 I've got terrible toothache. The dentist says he'll have to _____ my tooth.

Writing guide
Formal and informal messages

● Decide what sort of message you want to write. Is it formal or informal?

● Greet the person you're writing to:

Dear President ... (surname) = formal
Dear Mr/Mrs/Miss/Ms ... (surname) = formal
Dear ... (first name)
Hi ... (first name)

● Write a short message.

I'm writing because ...
I'd like to tell/ask you ...
I just want to say that ...

● Finish with:

Yours sincerely, ... = formal
Best wishes, ...
Love, ...

4 Writing *Your message*

Use what you know

Think of a person that you'd like to send a message to: a politician, an actor, a well-known person in your country, or someone you already know. Write your message on a piece of paper and give it to your teacher.

Then take someone else's message and imagine that you're the person it was written to. Write a reply and give it to the person who sent the message.

*We, the authors, would love to get a message from you! If you have time, write to us and tell us if you have enjoyed using **Messages**. We hope you have!*

Extra exercises

1 Read the text. Put the letters in the right order and make words connected with money.

My older brother Alex is useless with money. As soon as he's got some money in his wallet, he wants to [1]ndeps it. His [2]knab uncotca is always empty so he can't use the [3]coptihans, and he hasn't got a [4]tidrec drac any more. At work they pay him every Friday, but a few days later he's [5]kebor and he always tries to [6]worbro money from his friends – or from me! I know he'll give back the money, so I sometimes [7]nedl him something. On Thursdays he might have a little bit of [8]gencha in his pocket. But on Fridays he always walks to work because he can't [9]doffra a bus ticket.

2 Choose the right verb.

1 Was Matt upset? What did he (*say / tell*)?
2 Julia has lent her printer to Mike. She'll (*get / give*) it back next week.
3 I'm broke. Would you (*borrow / lend*) me some money?
4 Isobel (*told / said*) me that you wanted to see me.
5 How many foreign languages can you (*talk / speak*)?
6 Tom (*said / told*) that he was going to retire.
7 I've lent Mike £50. I hope he'll (*give / get*) it back.
8 Could you (*speak / say*) that again more slowly, please?
9 I really like Jane but she (*talks / speaks*) too much.

3 Complete the reported sentences with the right form of the verb.

1 STAVROS: I'm Greek.
   Stavros told us he _____ Greek.
2 BEN: I can't afford a new computer.
   Ben said that he _____ afford a new computer.
3 KATE: I'll be 18 in December.
   Kate told me she _____ 18 in December.
4 LISA: I borrowed some money.
   Lisa said that she _____ some money.
5 PETER: My parents have just come home.
   Peter said that his parents _____ just _____ home.
6 JUDITH: We didn't spend much money.
   Judith told me that they _____ much money.

4 Write what the people said.

1 *'My motorbike is a Harley-Davidson.'*

1 Andy told me that his motorbike was a Harley-Davidson.
2 Mrs Pringle said that her parrot could sing pop songs.
3 Nadia said she was writing to her cousin in Poland.
4 Danny said that his sister had an interesting job.
5 Mr and Mrs Todd told Danny they'd enjoyed the party on Saturday.
6 Karim told us he wouldn't be able to go to Pakistan this year.
7 Clare said she'd opened her bank account in July.
8 Luke said that he hadn't been to the leisure centre recently.

5 Complete the conversations. Choose from a–h.

1 A: Mum, I'm leaving now. I'm going to a party at Kerry's place.
   B: OK, then. _____
   A: Thanks. Bye!
2 A: Bye! See you on Monday.
   B: Yes. _____
3 A: Hello, Jamie.
   B: Oh, Kim, hi! _____ Come in!
4 A: Those cakes look nice. Can I have one?
   B: Yes, of course. _____
5 A: Well, I must go. Thanks for having me. _____
   B: I'm glad you enjoyed it. See you soon.

a Enjoy yourself.
b I've had a great time.
c Don't worry. Relax!
d Have a good weekend.
e Nice to see you.
f Sorry, but I can't come.
g Help yourself.
h I hope he had a good holiday.

6 How do you say these sentences in your language?

1 I'm broke.
2 We can't afford a new car.
3 Thanks for inviting us.
4 Nice to see you.
5 Turn the music down!
6 Enjoy yourself!

Extra reading

Keeping in touch

Think of some of the important developments in the history of communication. Which ones were the most important?

1 The first form of writing, as far as we know, was developed about 5,000 years ago in Mesopotamia (now Iraq). It was called cuneiform and it was based on simple pictures.

2 The printing press was invented in the 15th century. It was one of the most important inventions in the history of communication because, for the first time, large numbers of people could read information and ideas in the form of books and newspapers.

3 The Pony Express, in the USA, used teams of horses and riders to take messages across the country. They rode from Missouri in the east to Sacramento, California – a distance of more than 3,000 kilometres. They changed horses every 16 to 24 kilometres and the journey took between 10 and 16 days.

4 In 1844 an American called Samuel Morse built the world's first telegraph line. For the first time it was possible to send messages quickly over a long distance, using electricity, and later, radio.

Operators used Morse code, which was based on dots (•) and dashes (−), for example, ●●● = S. The message SOS ('Save our souls') was often used by ships in danger.

●●● ━━━ ●●●

5 The first telephone, made in 1881, looked very different from the phones we use today. Its inventor, Alexander Bell, thought that only a few people would want to use one. At first, he did not realise that he had changed the way that people communicated for ever.

6 Today one of the easiest and quickest ways to send a message is 'texting'. Millions of text messages are sent every day.

What does this text message mean?

A FINAL THOUGHT

'The pen is mightier* than the sword.'

* stronger

What do you think this proverb means?

Task

Read the texts, then complete the information.

1 People have used different forms of writing for .... years.
2 Newspapers and books were made on a ....
3 The .... in the Pony Express were a bit like our postmen today.
4 Telegraph operators didn't speak. They used ....
5 The .... was invented by Alexander Bell.
6 .... is quick and easy, and young people use it all the time.

Grammar check

1 Past perfect
Work it out for yourself

Match sentences 1 and 2 with a and b. Then complete the explanation.

a Everyone left before I arrived.

b I arrived, then everyone left.

We use the .... to show that one past action happened **before** another.

1 *When I arrived, everyone **left**.*
(past simple)

2 *When I arrived, everyone **had left**.*
(past perfect)

Check that you can

● use the past perfect.

Make one sentence each time. Use *when* or *because* and the past perfect.

1 *I went to bed when I'd done my homework.*

1 I went to bed. I did my homework. (*when*)

2 I felt more relaxed. I had a hot shower. (*when*)

3 Zoe was fed up. She lost her camera. (*because*)

4 The house was quiet. Everyone went to bed. (*because*)

5 Joe was upset. Someone stole his wallet. (*because*)

6 I bought a new tennis racket. I saved enough money. (*when*)

7 Anne was annoyed. No one did the washing up. (*because*)

8 She showed me the letter. She read it. (*when*)

2 *must, can't, might, could* for speculation
Work it out for yourself

1 He must be strong.

2 She can't feel very relaxed!

3 He might have/ could have a rabbit under his hat.

Read the explanations, then match Amy, Tara and Mel with sentences 1–3 above.

Amy thinks that something is impossible.
Tara thinks that something is possible, but she isn't sure.
Mel thinks that something is definitely true.

Check that you can

● express speculation.

Complete the sentences. Use *might/could, can't, must*.

1 I don't want to drink the water in the river. It _might/could_ be polluted.

2 Why are you buying that awful T-shirt? You .... be crazy.

3 You .... be tired. You've just slept for ten hours!

4 Don't eat those mushrooms. They .... be poisonous.

5 Annie .... be 15. She drives a car. She .... be at least 17.

6 Sit down and relax. You .... be tired.

7 Those glasses .... be Jasmine's. She doesn't wear glasses.

8 A: Listen. There's someone at the door.
   B: It .... be Nadia, or it .... be Clare.

3 Reported speech
Work it out for yourself

Direct speech	Reported speech
'I'm very happy.'	She said (that) she **was** very happy.
'We **aren't** selfish!'	He said (that) they **weren't** selfish.
'You **annoy** me!'	She said (that) I **annoyed** her.
'I **don't like** cats.'	He said (that) he **didn't like** cats.
'Jack **has gone** to Italy.'	She said (that) Jack **had gone** to Italy.
'I **haven't finished**.'	He said (that) he **hadn't finished**.
'I **saw** Helen in town.'	She said (that) she **had seen** Helen in town.
'Leo **didn't pass** the exam.'	He said (that) Leo **hadn't passed** the exam.
'The shops **will be** open at 8.30.'	She said (that) the shops **would be** open at 8.30.
'Chris **won't come**.'	He said (that) Chris **wouldn't come**.

Look at the table and complete this list of the changes from direct speech to reported speech.

1 *am/is/are* → ..*was/were*..
2 Present simple → ....
3 Present perfect → ....
4 Past simple → ....
5 *will/won't* → ..../.............

We sometimes use *that* before reported speech, but we often omit it.

Check that you can

● use reported speech.

Read what people said about a modern art exhibition in London. Then report what they said.

1 *Harry Price said it was the best thing in town.*

1 Harry Price: 'It's the best thing in town!'
2 Kate Steel: 'I really liked it.'
3 Joe Kelly: 'I've never seen such an awful exhibition.'
4 David Joplin: 'I'll never forget it.'
5 Tara Smith: 'I can't afford £15 for a ticket.'
6 John Frost: 'Modern art annoys me.'
7 Mary West: 'I won't go again.'
8 Paul Tate: 'I want to see it again.'

4 *say* and *tell*
Work it out for yourself

Look at the pictures and read the dialogue. Then complete the explanations, using *say* and *tell*.

Jack, how old are you?

I'm 16.

Jack, how old are you?

I'm 18.

GEMMA: *Jack **said** he was 16.*
KATE: *Really? He **told me** he was 18!*

1 We always use a noun/pronoun object after .... (*He told me. I told the teacher.*)
2 We don't use a noun/pronoun object after .... (**Not** *Jack said me.*)

Check that you can

● use *say* and *tell*.

Complete the sentences. Use *told* or *said*.

1 My sister ..*told*.. me it was a very good film. She .... I'd really like it.
2 I .... Maria that I wasn't free at the weekend.
3 The teacher .... us we could leave early.
4 Jack .... his cousin was a pop star, but everyone .... me that it wasn't true.
5 The police .... Joe they'd found his bike.
6 Dave .... me he was broke, so I .... I could lend him some money.

Vocabulary and expressions

Feelings
annoyed
disappointed
embarrassed
fed up
lonely
nervous
pleased
relaxed
relieved
surprised
upset
worried

In the mountains
(to) crawl
crevasse
disaster
foot (of a mountain)
guilty
(to) hop
ice
icy
(to) lower
(to) manage to ...
pain
precipice
(to) reach
(to) risk
rope
weight

Adverbs
angrily
early
fast
hard
late
loudly
nervously
quickly
recently
sadly
safely
slowly
successfully
well

Money
(to) afford
bank account
(to) be broke
(to) borrow
cashpoint
change
credit card
(to) lend
(to) spend

Everyday expressions
Enjoy yourself.
Have a good holiday.
Help yourself.
Nice to see you.
We had a great time.

Messages
current (n.)
detail
(to) float
marine scientist
payment
pirate
post (n.)
regularly
smoke signals
tiny

Phrasal verbs
(to) find out
(to) give up
(to) grow up
(to) pick up
(to) put on
(to) take off
(to) take out
(to) turn down
(to) turn off
(to) turn on

Study skills 6
Learning English on your own

You've spent a long time studying English. Don't waste it! Here are some things you could do to continue practising your English. Read the list and put the eight items in your 'order of probability'. Which things will you definitely do? Which things might you do? Which things won't you do?

1 Exchange emails or chat on the Internet in English.
2 Listen to English programmes on the radio.
3 Read English magazines and newspapers.
4 Watch English films.
5 Listen to songs in English.
6 Read websites in English.
7 Write new words in a vocabulary notebook.
8 Talk to people from other countries in English.

Work with a friend and compare your ideas.

> I don't expect I'll read any English newspapers.

> I'll definitely listen to English pop songs.

How's it going?

● Your rating

Look again at pages 132 and 133. For each section decide on your rating: Good ✓✓✓   Not bad ✓✓   I can't remember much ✓

● Vocabulary

Look at the Vocabulary list and choose three words or phrases which might be useful if you travel to an English-speaking country. Share your ideas with the class and say when you would use these words.

● Test a friend

Look again at Units 11 and 12. Think of at least two questions, then ask a friend.

> What happened to Shelley Wood's house?

> Why did the Grays have a party?

● Correcting mistakes

Can you correct these mistakes? In some sentences, there is more than one mistake.

1 Julie mustn't be here; she said me she was going to London today.
2 Sam told that he didn't like prawns.
3 We arrived late to the cinema and the film started.
4 'I don't feel very relax.' 'Neither I do.'
5 I said him about our holiday and we passed a great evening.

● Your Workbook

Complete the Learning Diaries for Units 11 and 12.

Coursework 6 Our school magazine

Read the sports reports in this month's edition of *Pulse*. Then choose at least one sport and write a report about people and events in your community or country.

Sports News

ATHLETICS

Congratulations to all the students who represented Greenside at the Northwest Championships last week. Our long jump team did well and Sam Perch finished third in the Under-13s. Hayley Borne came second in the Junior Girls' 1500m and Richard Wilson won the Senior Boys' 800m. Richard is going to represent the Northwest in the National Championships next month. When *Pulse* spoke to him, he said he trained every day and he was feeling great. Good luck, Richard!

CRICKET

Unfortunately, several matches were cancelled because of the weather but the Greenside Cricket Team managed to win five of their eleven matches this season. Everyone enjoyed their trip to Somerset, with a win against a very strong team from Frome Community College. Special thanks to Mr Harris, Mr Hartigan and Mr Peach for their sense of humour, enthusiasm and patience!

HOCKEY

One of our star players, Rosie Moore, is spending a week at the Centre of Excellence at Milton School in August. She told us she was a bit nervous but she was really looking forward to it. We've asked her to write a report of her visit for next term's edition of *Pulse*.

FOOTBALL

The football season will begin again soon so get your boots out! If you would like to play for the school, there are four teams – Under 14, Under 15, Under 16 and Under 19. Trials will begin next Saturday: 10 am on the sports field. Football must be the most popular sport in the school, so make sure you get there early!

Grammar index

Communicative functions index

Unit 1
- Describe the present and the past *The man in the blue suit is Humphrey Bogart. He was born in New York.*
- Describe a picture *Three people are sitting at the counter.*
- Talk about famous people in the past *James Dean died in a car accident in 1955.*
- Contradict someone *You're always late! – No, I'm not!*
- Make a conversation about going out with friends *Who are we waiting for?*

Unit 2
- Talk about where you live *I live in a block of flats.*
- Describe people and things *We've got a neighbour who plays in a band.*
- Ask for clarification *Are they the ones with the parrot?*
- Guess what things are *Is he the one who lived in Spain?*

Unit 3
- Describe events in the past *He was playing baseball when the ball hit him.*
- Show interest and surprise *You're joking!*
- Talk about coincidences *We found out that we lived in the same street.*
- Describe things that you imagine and worry about *My friend Jess worries about everything.*
- Describe things that happened in the past and don't happen now *I used to walk in my sleep.*

Unit 4
- Talk about journeys and different forms of transport *It's cheaper if you go by coach.*
- Make travel arrangements *How long does it take?*
- Book a trip *I'd like to book a flight to Paris.*
- Say when and where things are/were done *The first jeans were made by Levi Strauss.*

Unit 5
- Describe recent events and give your news *Winston and Lorina have had another baby.*
- Describe recent news events *The President of the World Bank has arrived in London.*
- Talk about things people have and haven't done *We haven't had our results yet.*
- Offer to help *Shall I do the washing up?*
- Make suggestions *We could buy her some flowers.*

Unit 6
- Talk about things in the present that started in the past *He's lived there for 12 years.*
- Give details about your background *I was born in Verona 15 years ago.*
- Talk about your possessions *My father gave me this watch.*
- Describe important things and events *It's the most exciting thing I've ever done.*

Unit 7
- Describe special occasions *We had fireworks on my last birthday.*
- Talk about results *If you ring me from the station, I'll come and meet you.*
- Talk about superstitions *If you blow out all the candles, your wish will come true.*
- Talk about events in the future and future plans *I'll get the cake. It'll be ready tomorrow. Our neighbours are going to move to Italy.*
- React to what other people say *Is Andy coming tomorrow? I hope so.*

Unit 8
- Talk about things that aren't certain *I may/might go abroad next week.*
- Talk about what's right and wrong *You should always tell the truth.*
- Talk about hypothetical situations *I would give my honest opinion if a friend asked for advice.*
- Respond to opinions *That's true, but …*

Unit 9
- Talk about being in a group *I'm in the choir at school.*
- Describe your likes and dislikes *I can't stand cooking.*
- Describe your strengths and weaknesses *I'm useless at making decisions.*
- Ask people to do things *I want you to stand closer to Nadia.*
- Make polite requests *Would you mind opening the door?*
- Respond to requests *Of course not. No problem.*

Unit 10
- Talk about things you'd like to change *I'd like more holidays and less homework.*
- Talk about quantity *There was no fruit.*
- Express preferences *I'd prefer to play tennis tomorrow.*
- Ask different types of question *What eats frogs? What do frogs eat?*

Unit 11
- Describe events that happened before other events in the past *The storm had completely destroyed our house.*
- Talk about feelings *I still feel nervous when I hear the wind.*
- Talk about what you imagine is true *She must be 17 because she drives a car.*
- Show agreement and similarity *Neither am I. So do I.*

Unit 12
- Talk about money *I'm broke, as usual.*
- Report what people say *I said we'd sent them an invitation.*
- Make a conversation at a party *Hi. Come in! Nice to see you.*
- Use everyday expressions *Have a good holiday.*

Wordlist

Abbreviations   *adj* = adjective   *Amer* = American English   *n* = noun   *prep* = preposition   *v* = verb
colloq = colloquial   1.2 = Unit 1, Step 2   CW1 = Coursework, Module 1

A

accent /'æksənt/ CW1
accept /ək'sept/ CW2
across /ə'krɒs/ 4.3
active /'æktɪv/ 3.3
adapt /ə'dæpt/ 6.3
add up /æd ʌp/ 10.1
admire /əd'maɪə/ 8.3
admit /əd'mɪt/ 8.2
advice /əd'vaɪs/ 8.2
afford /ə'fɔːd/ 12.1
African /'æfrɪkən/ 1.3
afterwards /'ɑːftəwədz/ 7.3
(a long time) ago /ə'gəʊ/ 6.1
alive /ə'laɪv/ 5.3
along /ə'lɒŋ/ 4.3
amazed /ə'meɪzd/ 10.3
amazing /ə'meɪzɪŋ/ 10.3
amount /ə'maʊnt/ 5.2
angrily /'æŋgrɪli/ 11.3
annoyed /ə'nɔɪd/ 10.3
annoying /ə'nɔɪɪŋ/ 10.3
ant /ænt/ 9.3
argue about /'ɑːgjuː ə'baʊt/ 1.2
as (*conj*) /æz, əz/ 3.3
ash /æʃ/ 5.3
at first /ət 'fɜːst/ 3.3
audience /'ɔːdiəns/ 9.1
Austrian /'ɒstriːən/ 1.1
autobiography /ˌɔːtəʊbaɪ'ɒgrəfi/ 8.1
(be) away from /ə'weɪ frɒm/ 6.3

B

(at the) back /bæk/ 2.1
(the) back of /bæk əv/ 7.2
backpacker /'bækpækə/ 4.3
balcony /'bælkəni/ 2.1
band /bænd/ 9.1
bank (of a river) /bæŋk/ 4.3
bank account /bæŋk ə'kaʊnt/ 12.1
bean /biːn/ 10.1
because of /bɪ'kɒz əv/ CW6
believe in /bɪ'liːv ɪn/ 3.2
bell /bel/ 7.2
beside /bɪ'saɪd/ 9.3
best-selling /ˌbest'selɪŋ/ 10.3
bike ride /'baɪk raɪd/ 4.3
bleed /bliːd/ 3.1
block of flats /ˌblɒk əv 'flæts/ 2.1

blow out /bləʊ aʊt/ 7.1
bomb (*v*) /bɒm/ CW2
bone /bəʊn/ 5.2
book (*v*) /bʊk/ 4.1
bored /bɔːd/ 10.3
boring /'bɔːrɪŋ/ 10.3
borrow /'bɒrəʊ/ 12.1
boulevard /'buːləvɑːd/ 1.1
brave /breɪv/ 9.3
break a promise /breɪk ə 'prɒmɪs/ 8.2
break the law /breɪk ðə 'lɔː/ 8.2
breathing /'briːðɪŋ/ 3.3
bright /braɪt/ 12.2
broccoli /'brɒkəli/ 10.1
(be) broke /brəʊk/ 12.1
brush /brʌʃ/ 6.2
bullet train /'bʊlɪt treɪn/ 4.2
business /'bɪznɪs/ 6.1

C

cake /keɪk/ 7.1
cancel /'kænsl/ CW6
candle /'kændl/ 7.1
career /kə'rɪə/ 8.3
caretaker /'keəˌteɪkə/ CW1
carpenter /'kɑːpɪntə/ 9.1
carrot /'kærət/ 10.1
cart /kɑːt/ CW2
cashpoint /'kæʃpɔɪnt/ 12.1
catch fire /kætʃ 'faɪə/ 3.1
celebrate /'selɪbreɪt/ 7.1
celebration /ˌselɪ'breɪʃn/ CW2
chain /tʃeɪn/ 10.3
challenge (*n*) /'tʃælɪndʒ/ CW5
chance /tʃɑːns/ CW3
change (*n*) /tʃeɪndʒ/ 8.2
chapel /'tʃæpl/ 7.2
chase (*v*) /tʃeɪs/ 4.3
chat (*v*) /tʃæt/ 2.3
cheese /tʃiːz/ 10.1
chemicals /'kemɪklz/ 10.3
cheque /tʃek/ 8.3
chicken /'tʃɪkɪn/ 10.1
choir /'kwaɪə/ 9.1
client /'klaɪənt/ 8.1
club /klʌb/ 9.1
coincidence /kəʊ'ɪnsɪdəns/ 3.1
comb /kəʊm/ 6.2
come from /kʌm frɒm/ 1.2
come over /kʌm 'əʊvə/ 7.3

come true /kʌm 'truː/ 3.3
commentary /'kɒməntri/ 9.3
company /'kʌmpəni/ 4.2
con man /'kɒn mæn/ 8.3
condition /kən'dɪʃn/ CW5
confidence /'kɒnfɪdəns/ 2.3
confident /'kɒnfɪdənt/ 2.3
confused /kən'fjuːzd/ 6.3
Congratulations! /kənˌgrætʃʊ'leɪʃnz/ 7.1
control (*v*) /kən'trəʊl/ 2.3
convenient /kən'viːniənt/ 10.3
corridor /'kɒrɪdɔː/ 3.3
costume /'kɒstjuːm/ 7.1
counter /'kaʊntə/ 1.1
cover (*v*) /'kʌvə/ 3.3
crawl /krɔːl/ 11.3
creature /'kriːtʃə/ CW3
credit card /'kredɪt kɑːd/ 12.1
crevasse /krə'væs/ 11.3
crime /kraɪm/ 5.1
crocodile /'krɒkədaɪl/ 9.3
crowd /kraʊd/ 9.1
current (*n*) /'kʌrənt/ 12.3

D

damage /'dæmɪdʒ/ 10.1
decorations /ˌdekə'reɪʃənz/ 7.1
deep /diːp/ 3.3
defeat (*v*) /dɪ'fiːt/ CW3
defend /dɪ'fend/ 9.3
definitely /'defɪnətli/ 6.2
delighted /dɪ'laɪtɪd/ 8.3
deposit (*n*) /dɪ'pɒzɪt/ 8.3
depressed /dɪ'prest/ 10.3
depressing /dɪ'presɪŋ/ 10.3
detail /'diːteɪl/ 12.3
diner /'daɪnə/ 1.1
direct (*adj*) /daɪ'rekt/ 4.1
disappointed /ˌdɪsə'pɔɪntɪd/ 11.1
disaster /dɪ'zɑːstə/ 11.3
disguise /dɪs'gaɪz/ 8.1
dislike (*v*) /dɪ'slaɪk/ 9.1
distance /'dɪstəns/ 10.1
doorbell /'dɔːbel/ 12.2
down /daʊn/ 4.3
dragon /'drægn/ 3.2
dream about /driːm ə'baʊt/ 3.2
during /'djʊərɪŋ/ 6.1

E

early /'ɜːli/ 11.3
earrings /'ɪərɪŋz/ 6.2
earthquake /'ɜːθkweɪk/ 5.3
edition /ɪ'dɪʃn/ CW1
embarrassed /ɪm'bærəst/ 11.1
emigrate /'emɪgreɪt/ 6.1
(in the) end /end/ 4.3
(be) engaged /ɪn'geɪdʒd/ 2.2
engagement ring /ɪn'geɪdʒmənt rɪŋ/ 6.2
enjoy /ɪn'dʒɔɪ/ 9.1
Enjoy yourself. /ɪn'dʒɔɪ jɔː'self/ 12.2
enthusiasm /ɪn'θjuːziæzm/ CW6
environment /ɪn'vaɪərənmənt/ 5.1
erupt /ɪ'rʌpt/ 5.3
eruption /ɪ'rʌpʃn/ 5.3
evacuate /ɪ'vækjueɪt/ CW2
everyone /'evriwʌn/ 1.3
evil /'iːvl/ CW3
Exactly! /ɪg'zæktli/ 8.2
excited /ɪk'saɪtɪd/ 10.3
exciting /ɪk'saɪtɪŋ/ 10.3
expect /ɪk'spekt/ 12.1

F

fall off /fɔːl ɒf/ 4.3
famine /'fæmɪn/ CW4
famous people /'feɪməs 'piːpl/ 5.1
fancy dress /'fænsi dres/ 7.3
fascinated /'fæsɪneɪtɪd/ 5.3
fascinating /'fæsɪneɪtɪŋ/ 10.3
fashion /'fæʃn/ CW4
fast /fɑːst/ 11.3
fat (*n*) /fæt/ 10.3
(in) favour of /'feɪvər əv/ 10.3
fear /fɪə/ 3.3
fed up /ˌfed 'ʌp/ 11.1
feel at home /ˌfiːl ət 'həʊm/ 6.3
feel nervous /fiːl 'nɜːvəs/ 3.2
finally /'faɪnəli/ 3.3
find out /faɪnd aʊt/ 12.3
fireworks /'faɪəwɜːks/ 7.1
first floor /'fɜːst flɔː/ 2.1
float /fləʊt/ 12.3
following /'fɒləʊɪŋ/ 4.2
foot (of a mountain) /fʊt/ 11.3
for ages /fər 'eɪdʒɪz/ 6.1

foreigner /ˈfɒrənə/ 6.3
form (v) /fɔːm/ 4.2
fortnight /ˈfɔːtnaɪt/ 6.1
fountain /ˈfaʊntɪn/ 8.3
fox /fɒks/ 9.3
freedom /ˈfriːdm/ 3.3
fresh /freʃ/ CW1
frighten /ˈfraɪtn/ 3.2
from /frɒm/ 4.3
fuel /ˈfjuəl/ 10.1
full moon /fʊl ˈmuːn/ 1.3
full of /fʊl əv/ 3.1

G

gang /gæŋ/ 9.1
garage /ˈgærɪdʒ/ 2.1
garden /ˈgɑːdn/ 2.1
gas mask /ˈgæs mɑːsk/ CW2
generosity /ˌdʒenəˈrɒsɪti/ 2.3
generous /ˈdʒenərəs/ 2.3
get (something) back /get bæk/ 12.1
get on well with /get ɒn wel wɪð/ 2.3
get rich /get ˈrɪtʃ/ 7.1
get something right /get ˌsʌmθɪŋ ˈraɪt/ 10.2
geyser /ˈgiːzə/ 5.3
giant (adj) /ˈdʒaɪənt/ 5.3
give back /gɪv bæk/ 8.2
give up /gɪv ʌp/ 12.3
god /gɒd/ 3.3
Good luck! /gʊd ˈlʌk/ 7.1
good at /ˈgʊd ət/ 9.1
grab /græb/ 3.2
ground floor /ˈgraʊnd flɔː/ 2.1
grow up /grəʊ ʌp/ 12.3
guard (v) /gɑːd/ 3.3
guest /gest/ 7.1
guilty /ˈgɪlti/ 11.3

H

halfway /ˌhɑːfˈweɪ/ 1.3
Happy anniversary /ˈhæpi ˌænɪˈvɜːsəri/ 7.1
Happy birthday /ˈhæpi ˈbɜːθdeɪ/ 7.1
Happy New Year /ˈhæpi njuː ˈjɪə/ 7.1
harbour /ˈhɑːbə/ 8.3
hard /hɑːd/ 11.3
hate (v) /heɪt/ 9.1
Have a good holiday. /hæv ə gʊd ˈhɒlɪdeɪ/ 12.2
have nightmares /hæv ˈnaɪtmeəz/ 3.2
headphones /ˈhedfəʊnz/ 1.3
health /helθ/ 5.1
heartbeat /ˈhɑːtbiːt/ 3.3
heating /ˈhiːtɪŋ/ CW1

helmet /ˈhelmət/ 4.2
Help yourself. /help jɔːˈself/ 12.2
honest /ˈɒnɪst/ 2.3
honesty /ˈɒnəsti/ 2.3
hop /hɒp/ 11.3
hot spring /hɒt ˈsprɪŋ/ 5.3
How can I get to ...? /haʊ kæn aɪ ˈget tə/ 4.1
How far is it? /haʊ ˈfɑːr ɪz ɪt/ 4.1
How long does it take? /haʊ lɒŋ dʌz ɪt ˈteɪk/ 4.1
How weird! /haʊ ˈwɪəd/ 3.2

I

I agree /aɪ əˈgriː/ 8.2
I can't stand... /aɪ kɑːnt ˈstænd/ 9.1
I guess not. /aɪ ˈges nɒt/ 7.2
I guess so. /aɪ ˈges səʊ/ 7.2
I hope not. /aɪ ˈhəʊp nɒt/ 7.2
I hope so. /aɪ ˈhəʊp səʊ/ 7.2
I'd rather ... /aɪd ˈrɑːðə/ 10.1
ice /aɪs/ 11.3
icy /ˈaɪsi/ 11.3
I'm afraid I ... /aɪm əˈfreɪd aɪ/ 7.3
image /ˈɪmɪdʒ/ 3.3
imaginary /ɪˈmædʒɪnəri/ 3.2
increase (v) /ˈɪŋkriːs/ 5.3
independence /ˌɪndɪˈpendəns/ 2.3
independent /ˌɪndɪˈpendənt/ 2.3
interest (n) /ˈɪntrəst/ CW4
interested /ˈɪntrəstɪd/ 10.3
interesting /ˈɪntrəstɪŋ/ 10.3
into /ˈɪntə/ 4.3
It sounds (funny) /ɪt ˈsaʊndz/ 1.3
It takes (an hour) /ɪt ˈteɪks/ 4.1
It's in my blood. /ɪts ɪn maɪ ˈblʌd/ 6.3

J

jaws /dʒɔːz/ 9.3
joke (v) /dʒəʊk/ 1.2
junk food /ˈdʒʌŋk fuːd/ 10.3

K

keen on ... /kiːn ɒn/ 9.1
keep a promise /kiːp ə ˈprɒmɪs/ 8.2
keep a secret /kiːp ə ˈsiːkrət/ 8.2
key ring /ˈkiː rɪŋ/ 6.2
killer /ˈkɪlə/ CW3
kind /kaɪnd/ 2.3
kindness /ˈkaɪndnəs/ 2.3

L

label (n) /ˈleɪbəl/ CW2
last (v) /lɑːst/ 4.3
late /leɪt/ 11.3
later /ˈleɪtə/ 3.3
laugh (n) /lɑːf/ 9.1
leisure centre /ˈleʒə ˌsentə/ 5.1
lend /lend/ 9.2
less /les/ 2.3
Let me know. /let miː ˈnəʊ/ 7.3
lettuce /ˈletɪs/ 10.1
liar /ˈlaɪə/ 8.3
lifetime /ˈlaɪftaɪm/ 5.2
lift /lɪft/ 2.1
like (v) /laɪk/ 9.1
listen to /ˈlɪsn tə/ 1.2
lonely /ˈləʊnli/ 6.3
look after /lʊk ˈɑːftə/ 7.3
look at /lʊk ət/ 1.2
look for /lʊk fə/ 1.2
look forward to /lʊk ˈfɔːwəd tə/ 7.3
look round /lʊk raʊnd/ 7.3
look up (a word) /lʊk ʌp/ 7.3
lorry /ˈlɒri/ 4.2
lottery /ˈlɒtəri/ 12.1
loudly /ˈlaʊdli/ 11.3
low /ləʊ/ 1.3
lower (v) /ˈləʊə/ 11.3
loyal /ˈlɔɪəl/ 2.3
loyalty /ˈlɔɪəlti/ 2.3

M

make a mistake /meɪk ə mɪˈsteɪk/ 8.2
make a promise /meɪk ə ˈprɒmɪs/ 8.2
make sense /meɪk ˈsens/ 10.1
make sure /meɪk ˈʃɔː/ CW1
make up (v) /meɪk ʌp/ 3.2
make-up (n) /ˈmeɪkʌp/ 8.1
manage to ... /ˈmænɪdʒ tuː/ 11.3
marine scientist /məˈriːn ˈsaɪəntɪst/ 12.3
marriage /ˈmærɪdʒ/ 7.1
midday /ˌmɪdˈdeɪ/ 6.1
mind (n) /maɪnd/ 3.3
monument /ˈmɒnjʊmənt/ 8.3
most of /məʊst əv/ 5.2
mostly /ˈməʊstli/ 2.3
motorbike /ˈməʊtəbaɪk/ 4.2
move (house) /muːv/ 6.1
movement /ˈmuːvmənt/ 5.3
MP3 player /em piː θriː ˈpleɪə/ 6.2

N

nearby /ˌnɪəˈbaɪ/ 11.1
nervous /ˈnɜːvəs/ 11.1
nest /nest/ 9.3
nice and warm /naɪs ənd ˈwɔːm/ 1.3
Nice to see you. /naɪs tə ˈsiː juː/ 12.2
No way! /nəʊ ˈweɪ/ CW3
note (n) /nəʊt/ 7.3

O

official (adj) /əˈfɪʃl/ 8.3
old-fashioned /ˌəʊldˈfæʃnd/ CW4
one in a million /wʌn ɪn ə ˈmɪljən/ CW4
orchestra /ˈɔːkɪstrə/ 9.1
out of control /aʊt əv kənˈtrəʊl/ 3.3
outdoors /ˌaʊtˈdɔːz/ 7.3
over (= on top of) /ˈəʊvə/ 5.3
overlook /ˌəʊvəˈlʊk/ 2.1
overweight /ˌəʊvəˈweɪt/ 10.3
own (v) /əʊn/ 2.1

P

pain /peɪn/ 11.3
pan /pæn/ 3.1
parasite /ˈpærəsaɪt/ 9.3
parrot /ˈpærət/ 2.2
patience /ˈpeɪʃəns/ 2.3
patient (adj) /ˈpeɪʃənt/ 2.3
payment /ˈpeɪmənt/ 12.3
peace /piːs/ 5.1
pea /piː/ 10.1
petrol station /ˈpetrl steɪʃn/ 4.2
photo album /ˈfəʊtəʊ ˈælbəm/ 6.2
pick up /pɪk ʌp/ 7.2
pirate /ˈpaɪrət/ 12.3
plan (v) /plæn/ 4.3
play the part of /pleɪ ðə ˈpɑːt əv/ CW3
pleased /pliːzd/ 11.1
plenty of /ˈplenti əv/ Review 4
plover /ˈplʌvə/ 9.3
politics /ˈpɒlətɪks/ 5.1
post (n) /pəʊst/ 12.3
prawn /prɔːn/ 10.1
precious /ˈpreʃəs/ 6.2
precipice /ˈpresɪpɪs/ 11.3
prefer /prɪˈfɜː/ 9.1
prepare /prɪˈpeə/ 10.3
present (n) /ˈpreznt/ 7.1
pretend /prɪˈtend/ 3.2
private investigator /ˈpraɪvət ɪnˈvestɪˌgeɪtə/ 8.1

procession /prə'seʃn/ 7.1
product /'prɒdʌkt/ 10.3
properly /'prɒpəli/ 3.3
protection /prə'tekʃn/ 9.3
purse /pɜːs/ 6.2
put down /pʊt daʊn/ CW3
put on /pʊt ɒn/ 12.3

Q
quality /'kwɒliti/ 2.3
quickly /'kwɪkli/ 11.3

R
rain (n) /reɪn/ 11.1
reach /riːtʃ/ 11.3
really /'rɪəli/ 3.1
receipt /rɪ'siːt/ 8.3
receive /rɪ'siːv/ 11.1
recently /'riːsəntli/ 5.2
reception /rɪ'sepʃn/ 7.2
recognise /'rekəgnaɪz/ 12.2
recycling centre /ˌriː'saɪklɪŋ
   'sentə/ 5.2
regularly /'regjʊləli/ 12.3
relationship /rɪ'leɪʃnʃɪp/ 9.3
relax /rɪ'læks/ 7.2
relaxed /rɪ'lækst/ 11.1
relieved /rɪ'liːvd/ 11.1
reply (v) /rɪ'plaɪ/ 7.3
represent /ˌreprɪ'zent/ 5.2
request (v) /rɪ'kwest/ 7.3
respect (v) /rɪ'spekt/ 2.3
(the) rest of /'rest əv/ 8.1
retire /rɪ'taɪə/ 8.1
(in) return /rɪ'tɜːn/ 9.3
rice /raɪs/ 10.1
rider /'raɪdə/ 4.2
right now /raɪt 'naʊ/ 1.3
risk (v) /rɪsk/ 11.3
room (= space) /ruːm/ 7.2
rope /rəʊp/ 11.3
round /raʊnd/ 4.3
roundabout /'raʊndəˌbaʊt/ 4.2
RSVP /ˌɑːresviː'piː/ 7.3
rule (v) /ruːl/ 2.3
run out of (money) /rʌn aʊt
   əv/ 4.3

S
sadly /'sædli/ 11.3
safely /'seɪfli/ 4.3
satellite dish /'sætəlaɪt dɪʃ/
   5.2
scooter /'skuːtə/ 4.2
scream (v) /skriːm/ 11.1

sculpture /'skʌlptʃə/ 5.2
seasick /'siːsɪk/ 11.2
secretive /'siːkrətɪv/ 2.3
selfish /'selfɪʃ/ 2.3
selfishness /'selfɪʃnəs/ 2.3
senior (adj) /'siːniə/ CW6
sense of humour /sens əv
   'hjuːmə/ 2.3
sensitive /'sensɪtɪv/ 2.3
sensitivity /ˌsensɪ'tɪvɪti/ 2.3
series /'sɪəriːz/ CW3
sharp /ʃɑːp/ 9.3
shine (v) /ʃaɪn/ 7.2
shipyard /'ʃɪpjɑːd/ CW2
shocked /ʃɒkt/ 10.3
shocking /'ʃɒkɪŋ/ 10.3
since /sɪns/ 6.1
skill /skɪl/ 9.1.
slave /sleɪv/ CW4
sleep (n) /sliːp/ 1.1
slowly /'sləʊli/ 11.3
smell (n) /smel/ 10.3
smoke signals /'sməʊk
   sɪgnəlz/ 12.3
sociable /'səʊʃəbl/ 2.3
social system /'səʊʃəl
   'sɪstəm/ 9.3
soft drink /sɒft 'drɪŋk/ 10.3
soldier /'səʊldʒə/ 3.3
solve /sɒlv/ 9.1
someone /'sʌmwʌn/ 1.3
something /'sʌmθɪŋ/ 1.3
somewhere /'sʌmweə/ 1.3
specially /'speʃəli/ 10.3
species /'spiːʃiːz/ 9.3
speed limit /'spiːd ˌlɪmɪt/ 4.2
spend /spend/ 12.1
sport /spɔːt/ 5.1
stairs /steəz/ 2.1
strawberry /'strɔːbri/ 10.1
strength /streŋθ/ 9.1
successfully /sək'sesfəli/ 11.3
suddenly /'sʌdnli/ 3.3
suffer /'sʌfə/ CW3
suit (n) /suːt/ 1.1
sunset /'sʌnset/ 1.3
superstition /ˌsuːpə'stɪʃn/ 7.1
support (v) /sə'pɔːt/ 2.3
surfer /'sɜːfə/ 6.1
surprised /sə'praɪzd/ 11.1
symbol /'sɪmbəl/ 3.3

T
take off /teɪk ɒf/ 12.3
take out /teɪk aʊt/ 12.3

take part in /teɪk 'pɑːt ɪn/ 9.1
take-away food /teɪk ə'weɪ
   fuːd/ 10.3
talk about /tɔːk ə'baʊt/ 1.2
talk to /tɔːk tə/ 1.2
taste (good) (v) /teɪst/ 10.3
taste (n) /teɪst/ 10.3
team /tiːm/ 9.1
telepathic /ˌtelɪ'pæθɪk/ 3.1
tell lies /tel 'laɪz/ 8.2
tell the truth /tel ðə 'truːθ/
   8.2
That's strange! /'ðæts
   streɪndʒ/ 3.1
That's true! /'ðæts truː/ 8.2
then /ðen/ 3.2
the 1950s /ðə 'naɪntiːn
   'fɪftiz/ 1.1
think about /θɪŋk ə'baʊt/ 1.2
thought (n) /θɔːt/ 10.1
thoughtful /'θɔːtfəl/ 2.3
thoughtfulness /'θɔːtfəlnəs/
   2.3
throw away /θrəʊ ə'weɪ/ 5.2
tie (n) /taɪ/ 1.1
tiny /'taɪni/ 12.3
tornado /tɔː'neɪdəʊ/ 11.1
tour (n) /tʊə/ 1.3
tourist attraction /'tʊərɪst
   ə'trækʃn/ 8.3
toy (n) /tɔɪ/ 10.3
traffic lights /'træfɪk laɪts/ 4.2
trendy (colloq) /'trendi/ CW4
(sports) trial /'traɪəl/ CW6
tropical /'trɒpɪkl/ 9.1
(in) trouble /'trʌbl/ 3.1
trumpet /'trʌmpɪt/ 2.1
trust (v) /trʌst/ 8.2
tube /tjuːb/ 5.2
tuition /tju'ɪʃn/ CW5
turn down /tɜːn daʊn/ 12.3
turn into /tɜːn 'ɪntə/ 7.1
turn off /tɜːn ɒf/ 12.3
turn on /tɜːn ɒn/ 12.3
twin /twɪn/ 3.1

U
unadventurous
   /ʌnəd'ventʃərəs/ CW1
undergrowth /'ʌndəgrəʊθ/
   CW3
unfortunately /ʌn'fɔːtʃənətli/
   8.3
unless /ən'les/ 7.1

unnecessary /ʌn'nesəsəri/
   CW4
up /ʌp/ 4.3
upset (adj) /ʌp'set/ 11.1
useless at … /'juːsləs ət/ 9.1

V
vacuum cleaner /'vækjuːm
   'kliːnə/ 5.2
valley /'væli/ 4.3
valuable /'væljubl/ 6.2
violence /'vaɪələns/ CW4
vitamin /'vɪtəmɪn/ 10.1
vivid /'vɪvɪd/ CW2

W
wait for /weɪt fɔː/ 1.2
waitress /'weɪtrəs/ 1.1
wallet /'wɒlɪt/ 6.2
war /wɔː/ CW2
watch (n) /wɒtʃ/ 6.2
(in some) ways /weɪz/ 6.3
(on the) way to … /weɪ tə/ 4.3
We had a great time. /wiː
   hæd ə 'greɪt taɪm/ 12.1
weakness /'wiːknəs/ 9.1
weather /'weðə/ 5.1
weight /weɪt/ 11.3
weird /wɪəd/ 3.1
welcome (v) /'welkəm/ 7.3
well /wel/ 11.3
What a coincidence! /'wɒt ə
   ˌkəʊ'ɪnsɪdəns/ 3.1
What floor is it on? /wɒt 'flɔː
   ɪz ɪt ɒn/ 2.1
wheel /wiːl/ 4.2
when /wen/ 3.3
Which one … ? /wɪtʃ 'wʌn/
   2.2
while /waɪl/ 3.3
win (n) /wɪn/ CW6
wind (n) /wɪnd/ 11.1
wonder (v) /'wʌndə/ 1.3
wonderful /'wʌndəfəl/ 7.3
worried /'wʌrid/ 11.1
worry about /'wʌri ə'baʊt/ 3.2

Y
You're joking! /jʊə 'dʒəʊkɪŋ/
   3.1

Phonetic symbols

Consonants

/p/	pen	/s/	see	/ʒ/	usually
/b/	be	/z/	trousers	/dʒ/	generally
/t/	too	/w/	we		
/d/	do	/l/	listen		
/k/	can	/r/	right		
/g/	good	/j/	you		
/f/	five	/h/	he		
/v/	very	/θ/	thing		
/m/	make	/ð/	this		
/n/	nice	/ʃ/	she		
/ŋ/	sing	/tʃ/	cheese		

Vowels

/æ/	man
/ɑː/	father
/e/	ten
/ɜː/	thirteen
/ə/	mother
/ɪ/	sit
/iː/	see
/ʊ/	book
/uː/	food
/ʌ/	up
/ɒ/	hot
/ɔː/	four

Diphthongs

/eɪ/	great
/aɪ/	fine
/ɔɪ/	boy
/ɪə/	hear
/eə/	chair
/aʊ/	town
/əʊ/	go
/ʊə/	pure

Verb forms

Present simple

Affirmative	Negative	Question
I work	I don't work (I do not work)	Do I work?
You work	You don't work (You do not work)	Do you work?
He/She/It works	He/She/It doesn't work (He/She/It does not work)	Does he/she/it work?
We work	We don't work (We do not work)	Do we work?
You work	You don't work (You do not work)	Do you work?
They work	They don't work (They do not work)	Do they work?

Present continuous

Affirmative	Negative	Question
I'm working (I am working)	I'm not working (I am not working)	Am I working?
You're working (You are working)	You aren't working (You are not working)	Are you working?
He's/She's/It's working (He/She/It is working)	He/She/It isn't working (He/She/It is not working)	Is he/she/it working?
We're working (We are working)	We aren't working (We are not working)	Are we working?
You're working (You are working)	You aren't working (You are not working)	Are you working?
They're working (They are working)	They aren't working (They are not working)	Are they working?

Past simple

Affirmative	Negative	Question
I worked	I didn't work (I did not work)	Did I work?
You worked	You didn't work (You did not work)	Did you work?
He/She/It worked	He/She/It didn't work (He/She/It did not work)	Did he/she/it work?
We worked	We didn't work (We did not work)	Did we work?
You worked	You didn't work (You did not work)	Did you work?
They worked	They didn't work (They did not work)	Did they work?

Past continuous

Affirmative	Negative	Question
I was working	I wasn't working (I was not working)	Was I working?
You were working	You weren't working (You were not working)	Were you working?
He/She/It was working	He/She/It wasn't working (He/She/It was not working)	Was he/she/it working?
We were working	We weren't working (We were not working)	Were we working?
You were working	You weren't working (You were not working)	Were you working?
They were working	They weren't working (They were not working)	Were they working?

Future with *will*

Affirmative	Negative	Question
I'll work (I will work)	I won't work (I will not work)	Will I work?
You'll work (You will work)	You won't work (You will not work)	Will you work?
He'll/She'll/It'll work (He/She/It will work)	He/She/It won't work (He/She/It will not work)	Will he/she/it work?
We'll work (We will work)	We won't work (We will not work)	Will we work?
You'll work (You will work)	You won't work (You will not work)	Will you work?
They'll work (They will work)	They won't work (They will not work)	Will they work?

Present perfect

Affirmative	Negative	Question
I've worked (I have worked)	I haven't worked (I have not worked)	Have I worked?
You've worked (You have worked)	You haven't worked (You have not worked)	Have you worked?
He's/She's/It's worked (He/She/It has worked)	He/She/It hasn't worked (He/She/It has not worked)	Has he/she/it worked?
We've worked (We have worked)	We haven't worked (We have not worked)	Have we worked?
You've worked (You have worked)	You haven't worked (You have not worked)	Have you worked?
They've worked (They have worked)	They haven't worked (They have not worked)	Have they worked?

Past perfect

Affirmative	Negative	Question
I'd worked (I had worked)	I hadn't worked (I had not worked)	Had I worked?
You'd worked (You had worked)	You hadn't worked (You had not worked)	Had you worked?
He'd/She'd/It'd worked (He/She/It had worked)	He/She/It hadn't worked (He/She/It had not worked)	Had he/she/it worked?
We'd worked (We had worked)	We hadn't worked (We had not worked)	Had we worked?
You'd worked (You had worked)	You hadn't worked (You had not worked)	Had you worked?
They'd worked (They had worked)	They hadn't worked (They had not worked)	Had they worked?

Irregular verbs

Verb	Past simple	Past participle	Verb	Past simple	Past participle	Verb	Past simple	Past participle
be	was/were	been	fly	flew	flown	sell	sold	sold
beat	beat	beaten	forget	forgot	forgotten	send	sent	sent
become	became	become	get	got	got	shake	shook	shaken
begin	began	begun	give	gave	given	shine	shone	shone
bite	bit	bitten	go	went	gone/been	show	showed	shown
bleed	bled	bled	grow	grew	grown	sing	sang	sung
blow	blew	blown	hang	hung	hung	sink	sank	sunk
break	broke	broken	have	had	had	sit	sat	sat
bring	brought	brought	hear	heard	heard	sleep	slept	slept
build	built	built	hit	hit	hit	smell	smelt	smelt
buy	bought	bought	hold	held	held	speak	spoke	spoken
can/be able to	could	has/have been able to	keep	kept	kept	spend	spent	spent
			know	knew	known	stand	stood	stood
catch	caught	caught	leave	left	left	steal	stole	stolen
choose	chose	chosen	lend	lent	lent	swim	swam	swum
come	came	come	lose	lost	lost	take	took	taken
cost	cost	cost	make	made	made	teach	taught	taught
cut	cut	cut	meet	met	met	tell	told	told
do	did	done	pay	paid	paid	think	thought	thought
dream	dreamt	dreamt	put	put	put	throw	threw	thrown
drink	drank	drunk	read	read	read	understand	understood	understood
drive	drove	driven	ride	rode	ridden	upset	upset	upset
eat	ate	eaten	ring	rang	rung	wake	woke	woken
fall	fell	fallen	rise	rose	risen	wear	wore	worn
feel	felt	felt	run	ran	run	win	won	won
fight	fought	fought	say	said	said	write	wrote	written
find	found	found	see	saw	seen			

Songs

Unit 4 Blue savannah song

Blue savannah song
Oh, blue savannah song.
Somewhere 'cross* the desert
Sometime in the early hours
In a restless world
On the open highways.

My home is where the heart is.
Sweet to surrender to you only.
I send my love to you.

Blue savannah song
Oh, blue savannah song.
Racing 'cross the desert
At a hundred miles an hour
To the orange side
Through the clouds and thunder.

My home is where the heart is.
Sweet to surrender to you only.
I send my love to you.

I'm on my way back
And your love will bring me home.
I'm travelling fast
And your love will bring me home.
Will I discover
That your love will bring me home?

Somewhere 'cross the desert
Sometime in the early hours
To the orange side
Through the clouds and thunder.

My home is where the heart is.
Sweet to surrender to you only.
I send my love to you.

* across

Unit 7 Chapel of love

Chorus
We're going to the chapel
And we're gonna* get married.
Going to the chapel
And we're gonna get married.
Gee I really love you
And we're gonna get married.
Going to the chapel of love.

Spring is here, the sky is blue.
Birds will sing as if they knew.
Today's the day, we'll say 'I do'
And we'll never be lonely any more.

Chorus
Because we're ...

Bells will ring, the sun will shine.
I will be his, and he'll be mine.
We'll love until the end of time
And we'll never be lonely any more.

Chorus
Because we're ...

* going to

Unit 12 I can see clearly

I can see clearly now the rain has gone.
I can see all obstacles in my way.
Gone are the dark clouds that had me blind.
It's going to be a bright, bright sunshiny day.

I think I can make it now the pain has gone
All of the bad feelings have disappeared.
Here is my rainbow I've been praying for.
It's going to be a bright, bright sunshiny day.

Look all around, there's nothing but blue skies,
Look straight ahead, nothing but blue skies.

I think I can make it now the pain has gone.
And all of the bad feelings have disappeared.
I can see clearly now the rain has gone.
It's going to be a bright, bright
sunshiny day.